THE MOST INSPIRA
STORIES FOR YOUNG READERS

15

AMAZING & INSPIRING

TRUE TALES

FROM MODERN FOOTBALL GREATS

TERRENCE ARMSTRONG

CONTENTS

INTRODUCTION
MAKING THEIR FOOTBALL
DREAMS A REALITY

Football is known as America's pastime—and for good reason. The NFL is consistently ranked as the most popular sport in the US. Whether it's Monday Night Football or the Super Bowl, Americans live and breathe this game! There is just something captivating about two football teams facing off against each other, each side determined to carry the ball to the endzone and score for their team.

Football greats such as Peyton Manning, Troy Polamalu, Dan Marino, and Ben Roethlisberger—just to name a few—entirely dedicated themselves to the game. They did whatever they could to succeed. They all had their fair share of challenges along the way, but they did what they could to overcome them.

This book profiles a wide variety of football stars who have made names for themselves and have become some of the best players of all time. Thes football greats all have their unique strengths and weaknesses—and they've all learned plenty of valuable lessons along the way. Being successful in football takes skill, patience, and planning, just like most things in life. Keep reading to learn more about how these football greats found success and made their dreams a reality.

JEROME BETTIS
TAKING A RIDE ON THE BUS

Even as a rookie, Jerome Bettis stood out. This was particularly incredible, considering that he was initially a bit of a late bloomer when it came to football. In fact, he didn't start playing until his freshman year of high school!

Born on February 16, 1972, Jerome grew up in Detroit, Michigan, where he was the oldest child of Gladys Elizabeth and Johnnie E. Bettis. Due to chronic breathing issues, he was sidelined much of the time. He was diagnosed with asthma at the age of 14, which made him get winded easily when running. Thus, it wasn't surprising that Jerome was initially interested in activities where he could remain stationary. As it turns out, bowling was his favOrite sport early on.

His mom approved of the pastime. According to Jerome, "My mom started us bowling as a way to get us off the streets and get us doing something productive on a daily basis. It was a good outlet. Bowling kept us busy on the weekends, and schoolwork kept us busy during the week." Jerome was quite serious about bowling, and was just a kid when he won his first state bowling championship.

Bowling provided a good outlet for Jerome growing up, but there were still times when he managed to stray from the path. One incident, in particular, Jerome still remembers clearly. It was 1982, and arcade games like Pac-Man and Space Invaders were all the rage. One Saturday morning, Jerome wanted to play, but didn't have any quarters. He happened to notice a $20 bill nearly flopping out of his mom's purse, which was set on the table. He grabbed it and headed to the arcade.

That 20 dollars quickly turned into a lot of quarters, and Jerome spent the whole day blasting intergalactic bad guys to smithereens at the arcade. When he came home and tried to explain to his mother that he had only "borrowed" the 20 dollars, however, she really let him have it. She made Jerome realize that he had stolen the money from her, and that it was wrong to steal.

Jerome learned a couple of valuable lessons that day. The first was that a game of Space Invaders is not worth incurring the wrath of your mother. And the second was that it's just plain wrong to steal, so don't do it!

Jerome later credited his success with bowling for his later success with football. Even though the sports are vastly different from each other, his dedication to both was the same. It was the dedication he first developed at the bowling alleys that he later took with him to the football field.

But before he ever played on a football field, Jerome played on a football street! He first tossed around a football with neighborhood kids on the backstreets in Detroit. Jerome and his buddies turned the end of a street into their makeshift endzone and spent their days scoring touchdowns.

By the time he reached high school, Jerome realized that football had the potential to open doors for him. He knew that if he joined the high school team and did well, he just might get a scholarship to attend college. There weren't many college scholarships being offered for bowling (the first full bowling scholarship wasn't even offered until 1997), but there were certainly plenty of good scholarships out there for football players.

In order to help aid his progress toward this goal, a little bit of relocation was in order. He moved in with his aunt so that he could attend Henry Ford High School, which happened to have an excellent football program at the time. Jerome stayed with his aunt during the week and came home during the weekend.

The situation changed his sophomore year, when he was able to transfer to David MacKenzie High School, which was close to home. He had to keep his grades up to attend MacKenzie, so he studied hard while refining his skills on the field. The hard work paid off when he was named an All-American linebacker.

His senior year, Jerome's team won the West Division title for the entire Detroit Public School League. This championship meant that his reputation was solid by the time the college recruiters came around.

An invitation by Notre Dame in Indiana got Jerome's attention. This was due to the fact that they had a tradition of utilizing the fullback. In football, you have quarterbacks, halfbacks, and fullbacks. Quarterbacks are the most well-known and get most of the glory, but the other two positions are quite important, as well. The fullback is an aggressive member of the team who blocks opposing players and defends the quarterback and whoever else might have the ball. Thus, the fullback plays a crucial role in assisting the whole team. They often don't get the credit they deserve, but it's the fullback who smooths out the rough edges while plays are being executed.

Because Jerome knew that Notre Dame appreciated fullbacks, he decided to play for the school. His first season with Notre Dame took place in 1990, and saw him making a lot of adjustments in his approach. But this period of trial and error, he began to truly dominate during the 1991 and 1992 seasons.

Jerome was best known for his running game. Traditionally, the main emphasis for a fullback was blocking opponents and guarding the quarterback and running back, but Jerome proved that he could run the ball just as well as anyone else. Due to his running ability, Notre Dame began to use him in some fairly unique ways. In some plays, he was used as a diversion to keep the defense on their toes. For example, the quarterback would fake a handoff to Jerome and have him run as if his life depended on it. He was very convincing, and one time half the linemen for the other team chased him and tried to stop him and his phantom football. Meanwhile, the quarterback was free to either run the ball himself or throw a pass to an unguarded player.

Jerome had a great run with Notre Dame, but ultimately didn't finish his degree. Instead, he was drafted into the NFL during his senior year in 1993, when he was picked up by the St. Louis Rams. He played with the Rams for a few power-packed seasons before he was traded to the Pittsburgh Steelers in 1996.

At the time he was traded, the Steelers were a team in transition. This was before the days of Ben Roethlisberger. Back then, the Steelers were invested in a dynamic young quarterback named Kordell Stewart. Jerome was ready for a new start, and was happy to join the team.

The most intense game that first season with the Steelers was on November 4, 1996. In this game, Jerome had to face off against his former team, the Rams. Jerome felt that he needed to show his old teammates that he was in a better place, and he led the Steelers with a spectacular long drive to the end zone. His team ended up winning 42 to 6.

Named the NFL's MVP that 1996 season, Jerome seemed almost unstoppable. Once he was in motion, he was like a triple-decker bus rolling down the field. Soon enough, folks began to call him "The Bus" in recognition of that fact. But he wasn't without his weaknesses—and one particular weakness took him out for an entire game in 1997. That weakness was his asthma.

Jerome had struggled with breathing issues since he was a kid, and after one particularly rough tackle in 1997, he found himself entirely unable to breathe. He had just been slammed to the ground and had the wind knocked out of him. Football players get the wind knocked out of them all the time. They may be momentarily stunned, but they typically just get up and do what they can to catch their breath. What's not so common is having a player have the wind knocked out of them, and then be entirely unable to get their wind back.

Jerome couldn't get any air and felt as if he were suffocating to death. As is common with asthma, his bronchial tubes had constricted in such a way that no matter how hard he tried to breathe in, air would not come into his lungs. He was taken off the field in a stretcher to get treatment. A big part of that treatment was an asthma inhaler.

Anyone who has dealt with asthma has likely had a love-hate relationship with their inhaler. The inhaler itself seems just about useless most of the time—until the moment when you find that you need it. Suddenly, it becomes a lifeline. When an asthma sufferer feels like their entire lungs are about to collapse, a puff from an inhaler can do wonders.

Jerome once described the effect of his asthma on his game. "It bothers me sometimes. I have an inhaler on the sidelines in case I need it, and the doctors and trainers are there."

Despite this bit of adversity, Jerome was able to recover and come back strong—so strong, in fact, that he was once again named MVP. During that dynamic season, he also showed his dedication to giving back to the community by establishing his own charitable foundation called "The Bus Stops Here

Foundation." This organization seeks to uplift those who may feel left behind. This charitable organization has a special emphasis on aiding underprivileged kids.

By 2005, it was rumored that Jerome Bettis was thinking of retirement. But the Steeler's new quarterback, Ben Roethlisberger, had a heart-to-heart chat with Jerome. Ben promised him that if he stuck it out for one more season, he would make sure that the team made it to the Super Bowl.

Thanks to the efforts of both the Bus and Big Ben (as Ben Roethlisberger is called), this was a promise that was kept. In 2006, the Steelers won Super Bowl XL, a game that was held right in Jerome's backyard of Detroit. After this big victory, Jerome Bettis was able to retire on top and go out in style.

FIVE FUN FACTS

- Jerome Bettis was inducted into the "Pro Football Hall of Fame" in 2015.
- He rushed for over 13,000 yards during the course of his football career.
- Jerome Bettis played in the Pro Bowl six times.
- He went to college at Notre Dame University in South Bend, Indiana.
- He founded the "Bus Stops Here Foundation."

SOME TRIVIA!

Does he have a hobby?

He loves to bowl.

When did Jerome Bettis graduate from high school?

He graduated in 1990.

Did he play football in college?

Yes, he played for Notre Dame.

What's his hometown?

He grew up in Detroit, Michigan.

Did he have a nickname?

Yes! He was called "The Bus."

REAL-LIFE LESSONS

- Jerome Bettis didn't start playing football until his freshman year of high school. Even if you're a late bloomer, don't worry—you still have time for a course correction.
- Diversify your interests. Jerome Bettis was not only a football star—he also loved to bowl!

- Keep yourself busy. Whether he was playing football or bowling, Jerome Bettis always kept busy, and this kept him out of trouble.
- Persevere in the face of adversity. Jerome Bettis battled chronic asthma his whole life, but did his best to overcome this. Life isn't always perfect, but we have to make the best of it.
- Earn your own way in life. Don't steal! It's not worth provoking the wrath of your mother (as Jerome found out), and it's just plain wrong!

PEYTON MANNING
THE GAME MANNING BUILT

Despite being one of the greatest quarterbacks of all time, Peyton Manning is almost as well known for his charitable work as he is for his efforts on the football field. The Peyton Manning Children's Hospital is just one of many initiatives that he has taken part in since going pro. But long before he started playing in the NFL, Peyton was always a football player on a mission.

All the way back in prep school, when he was playing for Isidore Newman School in New Orleans, Louisiana, he was already dedicated to a worthy cause—his own older brother, Cooper Manning. Cooper might not be as well-known as his younger brothers, Peyton and Eli, but at one time he was an aspiring football player, as well. He was a highly competitive wide receiver at Newman. Unfortunately, his days on the field came to an end when he was diagnosed with spinal stenosis. This is an abnormal narrowing of the spinal canal that can cause one to lose feeling in their arms and legs.

This is an absolutely devastating condition for a football player, since they obviously can't throw a football if they can't feel their hands! Peyton understood just how devastated his brother Cooper was by this diagnosis, and began wearing his brother's jersey number (18) in his honor. Peyton wore this jersey his entire time at Isidore Newman, until he graduated in 1993 and went off to play college ball for the University of Tennessee.

Peyton played some exciting ball for Tennessee. In fact, the Tennessee Volunteers only lost six out of 45 games when he played with them. His efforts at Tennessee got him noticed, and in 1998 he was the first overall draft pick, by the Indianapolis Colts. There are times when a first pick can be overhyped, but in Peyton's case, he more than lived up to the expectations.

Peyton was NFL MVP in both 2003 and 2004. In 2005, the Colts made it to the playoffs, but fell short when they were trounced by the Pittsburgh Steelers. At this point in his career, folks began wondering if Peyton Manning could take it all the way. Could he win a Super Bowl?

Peyton entered the 2006 season determined to prove that he could do just that. The first game of that season had Peyton and the Colts facing off against the New York Giants, where his younger brother Eli was the quarterback. Peyton made sure to blow his little brother's team out of the water. This kicked off a winning streak for the Colts and they once again ended up in the playoffs, where they won a crucial game against the Kansas City Chiefs.

After beating the Chiefs, they took on the Baltimore Ravens, who they also handily dispatched. They had one more formidable obstacle in their path—the New England Patriots. The Colts and the Patriots had long been rivals, and during this fateful matchup, that rivalry was clearly on display. The Colts once again triumphed, with a 38 to 34 victory.

On February 4, 2007, Peyton led the Colts to a Super Bowl win against the Chicago Bears, 29 to 17. The Colts were the champions of Super Bowl XLI!

Coming off of this Super Bowl win, the Colts were eager to build upon their success. They began the 2007 regular season with seven wins, and were once again in a prime position to take on

NFL superstars, the New England Patriots. The Colts fought hard, but Patriots quarterback Tom Brady fought harder and led his team to victory, winning 24 to 20.

Peyton didn't seem to have as much momentum after this loss, and the Colts lost their next game to the San Diego Chargers. Then, they lost again to the Kansas City Chiefs. Peyton played poorly against the Chiefs, and didn't throw a single touchdown pass. Fortunately, the Colts were finally able to break out of their slump and ultimately finished the year atop the AFC South.

The 2008 season seemed to hold a lot of promise for the Colts, but ultimately stalled out due to Manning having to deal with an injured left knee. He was in a lot of pain and had to have an operation to remove a bursa sac that had become infected. After the surgery, he was forced to sit out several games to recover.

The 2009 season was better for Peyton. The Colts were in top form as they broke in the newly established football field of Lucas Oil Stadium—or, as Indianapolis Colts fans like to call it, the "house that Manning built." It's called this because folks in Indiana realize the great debt that they owe Peyton Manning for reinvigorating the Indianapolis team.

During the 2011 season, Peyton Manning was severely tested when he injured his neck. One injury led to another, and he was eventually diagnosed with a herniated disc that affected his throwing arm.

In the midst of this troubling injury, Peyton surely thought of his brother Cooper and how his own football career was ended due to similar neck problems. Was this the end of Peyton's career, too? He could only wonder.

Ultimately, Peyton recovered. He left the Colts, but rebounded with the Denver Broncos, who signed him to a $96 million dollar contract in 2012. He took the Broncos to the Super Bowl in 2014, but they ultimately lost to the Seattle Seahawks. Even so, Peyton was a good sport about it. He congratulated his opponents, and even stayed afterwards to sign autographs for fans. Many other players might have felt dejected and left as soon as possible. Likewise, some fair-weather quarterbacks may have chafed under the scrutiny after such a defeat. But not Peyton Manning. He was a big enough person to stick around and spend time with his supporters, even though he was sad about losing the championship.

Peyton Manning was frustrated at the loss, but he bounced back. He returned to the Super Bowl a couple of years later, in 2016, where he faced off against the Carolina Panthers. This time around, he was successful and led the Broncos to victory. With two Super Bowl rings on his fingers, Peyton Manning announced his retirement from football a short time later.

FIVE FUN FACTS

- In 2009, animated versions of all three Peyton brothers—Cooper, Peyton, and Eli—appeared on *The Simpsons*.
- In 1999, Peyton established the "PeyBack Foundation" aimed at giving back to the community—especially children growing up in poverty. Each Christmas, the PeyBack Foundation hosts the "PeyBack Holiday Celebration," where gifts are given to needy families.
- Peyton Manning holds the Colts' team record for the most passing yards in a single season.
- He was named the NFL MVP twice.
- Star Wars novelist Drew Karpyshyn once declared Peyton to be the "NFL personality most likely to become a Jedi Knight."

SOME TRIVIA!

In what year did Peyton Manning first play in a Monday Night Football game?

He first played in the year 2000.

Where did Peyton Manning go to college?

He attended the University of Tennessee.

Peyton was drafted in which pick in round one of the draft?

He was first pick.

What year was Peyton Manning drafted?

1998.

Did Peyton Manning ever play for the Baltimore Colts?

No! It's true that the Colts were once located in Baltimore, before they relocated to Indianapolis—but that was long before Peyton Manning's time with the team!

REAL-LIFE LESSONS

- Give back to the community. From the PeyBack Foundation and Peyton Manning Children's Hospital to raising awareness for his own brother Cooper's condition, Peyton has been a generous contributor to many worthy causes throughout his career.

- Be determined. Peyton showed fierce determination during his Super Bowl run in the 2006/2007 season.

- Stay positive. Peyton was disappointed when his performance suffered during his last few seasons with the Colts. He had to learn to pick himself up and start again—and so should you.

- Be a good sport. Peyton lost his first Super Bowl with the Broncos, but was still polite enough to sign autographs. Even when things don't turn out exactly as we want, we should still show respect and have good manners.

- Know how to leave on a high note! Peyton played for the mile-high city of Denver, Colorado, and knew how to go out on top. There's a beauty in making our exit gracefully from the various stages of our lives.

DAN MARINO
GREAT EVEN WITHOUT THE RING

Football legend Dan Marino was born on September 15, 1961, the son of hardworking Pittsburgh natives Veronica and Dan Marino Sr. By the time Dan Marino Jr. was in high school, he played both baseball and football—and excelled at both. In fact, he was actually drafted by the Kansas City Royals his senior year in the 1979 MLB draft. Marino ultimately declined, however, deciding to pursue a career in football.

There are times when life presents us with a fork in the road, and we must make a decision. The path that Dan chose led him to the University of Pittsburgh, where he played for the Pittsburgh Panthers from 1979 to 1982 as their star quarterback. Marino was a standout star on the team, and his teammates were pretty good, as well. The Panthers became one of the highest ranked college teams, but not everything always worked out as planned. There were definitely some mishaps along the way—mistakes that the Panthers' passionate fanbase didn't hesitate to point out.

Dan Marino's mom and dad often got an unwanted earful when they were in the stands at Pittsburgh Panther games, especially when fans didn't like something that Dan Marino did. His mother had a hard time dealing with all of the negative chatter and criticism she heard about her son, but his father took it all in stride. He felt it was a valuable opportunity for his son to learn how to take such harsh criticism and not let it get him down. The elder Marino was quick to point out to his son that everyone had their own personal opinions about how something should be approached. No matter what he might do, he would always have critics.

Dan's lackluster senior year attracted plenty of criticism, for this ended up being his worst season in college. Dan Marino later blamed much of this dismal season on a "coaching change" that had taken place. Whatever the case may be, the team hit a losing streak and Dan's last college football game was one of his worst. His team suffered a 7-3 defeat at the hands of Southern Methodist University, even though Southern Methodist was considered an underdog at the time. Nevertheless, Dan Marino later recalled that this incident taught him a valuable lifelong lesson: that sometimes in life you have to take the good with the bad. With the support of his friends, family, and teammates, Dan learned to persevere.

This hard-won patience served him well while he awaited the 1983 NFL draft. Dan was a college star and was fairly certain of his prospects, but things did not go exactly as he had hoped. He had expressed some interest in staying in Pittsburgh and playing for the Steelers. Growing up in Pittsburgh, Dan was a of course a big fan of the team. He had followed the Steelers all throughout the 197os and early 1980s. The Steelers were undisputed NFL champs at this time, having won a total of four Super Bowls. But they already had a full roster. They still had football legend Terry Bradshaw on the team, and had already recruited Mark Malone as a backup quarterback. Even though Dan was a local, the Steelers weren't interested in bringing him onto the team as their quarterback.

Several other notable players were chosen before Dan, who was finally tapped for the 27th pick during the first round, by the Miami

Dolphins. Dan Marino knew all about the Dolphins and their successes on the field, and was pleased to know that he had been recruited by a solid team with a history of winning. He was especially happy that his coach would be the legendary Don Shula.

Dan could have had a chip on his shoulder going into the 1983 season with the Dolphins, since he was such a late pick, but he instead decided to try even harder and prove his worth. He didn't want to let his fans down, he didn't want to let Shula down, and, most importantly, he didn't want to let himself down.

Dan later recalled that his 27th pick taught him to count his blessings, not complain, and do the best he could with what he had been given. He went into his first season determined to not only do well, but also to be a team player. He developed solid relationships with his coach and teammates in order to build an effective and solid team that was adept at winning football games.

The Dolphins played well during Dan's first few seasons, but they definitely had their ups and down. One of the ups (and subsequent downs) occurred on January 20, 1985, during Super Bowl XIX. It was a highlight of Dan Marino's career, due to the fact that he had made it to the Super Bowl. It would always haunt him, however, that his team came up short and failed to win during the big game.

Super Bowl XIX saw the Miami Dolphins take on their long-time nemesis, the San Francisco 49ers. The Dolphins played hard, but struggled to keep pace with their seasoned opponents. Ultimately, they were trounced by San Francisco's tremendous offensive capabilities. Led by the rocket reflexes of quarterback Joe Montanna, the San Francisco 49ers scored 38 points compared to the Dolphins' measly 16.

Even worse were the interceptions that Dan Marino threw, coupled with the fact that he was sacked a total of four times. If a quarterback gets sacked, it means that they held onto the ball just a bit too long and were tackled by members of the opposing team. This is not only bad for a team's objective of advancing the ball down the field, it can also lead to some pretty bad injuries. Quarterbacks train to quickly pass the ball down the field, not to sustain brutal tackles.

Dan had more than his fair share of injuries during the course of his career. In 1993, several seasons after that fateful Super Bowl loss, he received a pretty nasty injury to his Achilles tendon. He tore it so severely that he was on crutches for much of the rest of the season and unable to play. By the time the 1994 season rolled around, however, he was all healed up and on much better footing. Marino led the Dolphins to a 10-6 finish that year.

One of the most memorable games of the season was a nailbiter against the New York Jets, in which the Dolphins rallied to beat the Jets 28 to 24. The pivotal moment came when Dan Marino unleashed his secret weapon—The Clock Play. During this play, dan faked out the opposition with a fake spike, and ended up winning with a last-minute touchdown pass. As the clock ticked down to just 30 seconds remaining, Dan Marino acted as if he were going to spike the ball to set up a field goal that would have tied the game. But instead, he threw the ball to the right corner of the field and straight into the hands of Mark Ingram who proceeded to score the winning touchdown.

Just about everyone who saw this incredible play learned a valuable lesson: Expect the unexpected! They also learned that you can never completely count anyone out. As long as Dan Marino and his team were on the field and had a few seconds on the clock, they knew they could still win.

Later that year, Dan starred alongside another unlikely hero: comedian Jim Carey's character Ace Ventura. This classic comedy centered around Ace's work as a pet detective. In the film, Dan Marino and the Miami Dolphins' mascot, a dolphin named "Snowflake," go missing, and Ace Ventura comes to the rescue. The fact that Marino agreed to be in such a silly film demonstrates that he didn't take himself too seriously.

Dan Marino's last season was in 1999, as he retired in 2000. Even though he never won a Super Bowl, fans will always remember the incredible tenacity and ingenuity that he made use of during his time on the field.

FIVE FUN FACTS

- Dan Marino only played for the Miami Dolphins.
- He only appeared in one Super Bowl.
- Dan Marino was the first quarterback to throw for 60,000 passing yards.
- He was rarely sacked. In 1988, his sack percentage was 1%!
- He is often considered one of the best players to have never won a Super Bowl.

SOME TRIVIA!

What movie did Dan Marino appear in?

Ace Ventura Pet Detective.

What team did Dan Marino and the Dolphins lose to in their only Super Bowl appearance?

The San Francisco 49ers.

When was Dan Marino inducted into the Football Hall of Fame?

He was inducted into the Hall of Fame in 2003.

What pick was he in the first round of the NFL Draft?

Dan Marino was the 27th pick in the first round.

What year did Dan Marino almost make it to the Super Bowl?

In 1993, Dan Marino and the Miami Dolphins were within striking distance of another Super Bowl when Marino severely injured his Achilles tendon. This injury was a great setback, and possibly the reason Dan Marino never made another Super Bowl appearance.

REAL-LIFE LESSONS

- We all have to make some pretty important decisions in life. Dan Marino had to decide early on whether to accept an MLB draft or go to college. Just like Dan, you might find yourself faced with a tough decision. Weigh your options carefully, take your time considering your decision, and choose the path you think is best for your life.

- There are always going to be critics in life. Dan learned this lesson back when he played college ball for the Pittsburgh Panthers. His mom and dad often heard the harshest of critiques leveled at their son from the stands. Dan very quickly learned, however, that there will always be people who are critical of your performance, and that it is impossible to please everyone. Just like Dan, don't get discouraged in the face of criticism. Instead, just do the best that you can.

- Life has its ups and downs. Sometimes we win, and sometimes we lose. Dan realized this during a losing slump in his senior year of college. He didn't beat himself up over it. Instead, he learned that we have to sometimes take the good with the bad, and find the strength to move on.

- Being the 27th pick in the first round of the NFL draft was a frustrating experience for Dan Marino, but he decided to make the best of it. Instead of becoming bitter, he simply got better. He worked hard and proved that he was much better than anyone anticipated. He used adversity to power his own determination, and we should all learn to do the same.

- Dan learned to be a team player. He didn't hog the spotlight. Instead, he knew how to delegate tasks and established an organized group of players with unified principles and objectives. It was a winning formula for football, and it's a winning formula in life.

TROY POLAMALU
MR. HOT AND COLD

Troy Polamalu was born on April 19, 1981. He grew up in sunny California, in a single-parent household, since his dad split when Troy was just a small child. His mother, Suila Polamalu, did the best she could to make up for the fact that Troy's father wasn't around. Unfortunately, his home life remained a bit rocky, and Troy began to get into trouble at a young age.

According to some accounts, he was smoking by the age of eight, running with a rough crowd, and engaging in petty theft. That's certainly not a good start for any young person. At any rate, he was apparently quite a handful for his mother—so much so that Troy was eventually sent over to the home of an aunt and uncle who lived in Tenmile, Oregon.

The uncle—Salu Polamalu—was his mother's brother, and became determined to offer Troy Polamalu a course correction in his life. The biggest change was perhaps the setting itself, for the rural, small-town atmosphere of Tenmile was far different from the hectic city life that Troy had previously known.

This change of scenery seemed to do wonders for Troy. Instead of running the streets, he enjoyed playing in green pastures. Tenmile was also the place where Troy first honed his football skills. He played ball for Douglas High School, which was located in nearby Winston, Oregon. While at Douglas High, Troy became known for his large number of interceptions.

In football, when a player catches a pass thrown by the opposing team, it's called an interception. Normally, a player passes the ball to a fellow team member, but if a member of the opposition is skilled enough, they can snatch the ball out of the air before it reaches its target. Troy was quite good at this.

He was also a good student. He kept his grades up and gave his all to whatever he applied himself to. Out of all of his classes, he especially enjoyed wood shop. He loved crafting furniture, such as coffee tables and chests out of wood.

Troy graduated from Douglas High School in the 1999. Then, after accepting a scholarship to play for the University of Southern California, he continued to refine his unique skillset even further.

Along with studying and practicing hard on the field, Troy also explored his Polynesian heritage. His family originally hailed from American Samoa, and during his time at USC, Troy hooked up with a special Polynesian club on campus to learn and discuss more about Polynesian culture. He also brushed up on the Samoan language. All of this was quite beneficial when Troy made a trip out to American Samoa to spend time with his mom, who had since remarried and relocated to the region.

After college, Troy was drafted by the Pittsburgh Steelers in 2003. While playing in Pittsburgh, as a defensive back, he impressed fans, opponents, and teammates alike with his sheer ferocity on the field. Jerome Bettis once stated that Troy Polamalu had a kind of split personality, noting that he was as nice, polite, and as sweet as could be off the field, but turned into an "animal" on the field.

Troy admitted as much himself, stating that he worked hard to compartmentalize and separate the aggressiveness of football from the rest of his personal life. He believed that it was well and good to use football as an outlet for aggression, but that none of it should ever spill over outside of the game.

During his career, Troy was involved in the rise of Ben Roethlisberger and the Steeler's celebrated Super Bowl win in 2006. That year, the Steelers faced off against the Seattle Seahawks in the championship game. Troy played a big part in helping the Steelers make it to the Super Bowl in the first place, and during that fateful game, he showed up in a big way.

Like a human missile, he seemed to leap out of nowhere at times, taking out the opposing team's offense. He also put a lot of pressure on the Seahawks' quarterback Matt Hasselbeck, causing him to rush through his passes. This paid off in the last quarter, when Troy caused a harried Hasselbeck to botch a pass so badly that it was intercepted by Steelers player Ike Taylor.

Thanks to Troy Polamalu, the Steeler's defense was so solid that the Seahawks only managed to score one touchdown and one field goal the whole entire game. At the end of regulation time, the Steelers had 21 points and the Seahawks just 10.

Troy taught his teammates the meaning of giving it your all, and he did so with just about every move he made. His efforts helped the Steelers bag another Super Bowl victory in 2009. He continued to play several more seasons with the Steelers before retiring in 2013. Troy learned a lot during his legendary run, and he also taught a lot by way of his example.

FIVE FUN FACTS

- Troy played college ball for the University of Southern California.
- Troy Polamalu led the Steelers in interceptions twice.
- He was in the Pro Bowl eight times.
- Troy won the Defensive Player of the Year award in 2010.
- He participated in two Super Bowl wins.

SOME TRIVIA!

Does he have a nickname?

Yes, he's been given the nickname the "Tasmanian Devil" because of his wild, unpredictable moves on the field.

What position did Troy Polamalu play?

Troy was a defensive back.

How many Super Bowl rings does he have?

He has two.

Does he have any hobbies?

Troy Polamalu enjoys surfing.

What is his favorite food?

He loves fish—especially rainbow trout.

REAL-LIFE LESSONS

- Work hard at whatever you do. During his high school days, Troy Polamalu worked hard on the football field, in the classroom, and even in his wood shop class.
- Don't forget your roots. During his college days, Troy joined a special club dedicated to all things Polynesian. Troy learned to be proud of and embrace his culture.

- Due to his aggression on the field and polite nature off of it, Troy's teammates thought he had a split personality. In truth, Troy is just a master of self-control. He can turn on the energy and aggression when necessary, but can just as easily turn it off.
- Remain dedicated. Troy impressed everyone around him with how dedicated he was to putting everything he had into a football game. We, too, can apply this dedication to just about every aspect of our lives.
- During that fateful 2006 season that led the Steelers to the Super Bowl, Troy really showed his worth. He did everything he could to improve his team's chances of taking it all the way. Demonstrate how valuable you are, and you will be perceived as such.

I have included these free downloadable gifts to help light up your inner inspiration & reach your potential.

While you are reading through the stories, lessons and trivia, we recommend that you make use of all the bonuses we've attached here!

All our bonuses have been made specifically to help young athletes feel fired up, get inspired from the best to ever do it, and most importantly fall more in love with this incredible game!

Here's a list of what you're getting:

1) 250 Fun Facts From The World Of Sports
2) Sports Practice and Game Calendar
3) 5 Fun Exercise Drills for Kids
4) The BEST Advice From The Greatest Athletes Of All Time
5) The Mental Mindset Guided Meditation & Affirmation Collection
6) The Most Famous Events In Sports History And What They Can Teach Us

Now, it's over to you to scan the QR code, follow the instructions & get started!

BRET FAVRE
DOWN IN THE BAYOU

Brett Favre began life in Gulfport, Mississippi, where he was born on October 10, 1969, to Irvin and Bonita Favre. He grew up in a rural setting. But Brett wasn't brought up in midwestern cornfields. Instead, his stomping grounds were the swampy bayous of the southern gulf.

This distinction matters, because when he was a kid, Brett was more likely to see an alligator than a cow! At eight years old, he was playing in the backyard when he noticed a few alligators in a nearby stream. Brett got the bright idea to make some friends out of these gators. All friends like a good snack, so he quickly ran inside and grabbed some cookies. He tossed the baked goods to the gators in the water. To his delight, they lunged forward and snapped their jaws shut on the tossed cookies.

Thinking he had a winning formula for gator friendship, Brett began feeding the gators on a routine basis, and they came out like clockwork in anticipation of the human who dared to give them these sugary treats. But one day, his dad came home early. Brett knew he wasn't allowed to play with gators, so he stayed inside and refrained from his normal feedings. The gators wanted their routine snack, however, and started crawling toward the house in search of those tasty cookies. Irv took one look at the gators encroaching on his homestead, grabbed his shotgun, and started firing off shots. The gators got the message, and rushed back to the stream.

That afternoon, Irv had a stern talk with his son, and little Brett Favre promised to never feed the gators again. Brett was a rambunctious kid, but at the end of the day he respected his parents, so if they told him not to do something, he didn't do it.

Brett's parents were simple but hardworking people, and he was raised to value hard work and determination. He readily applied these ethics to football. Brett honed his football skills at the local high school, Hancock North Central, where he was on both the football and baseball teams. But it was his throwing arm on the football field that got the most attention.

Southern Mississippi coach Mark McHale took note of Brett's talent as a quarterback. McHale was in town scouting for prospects, and all it took was one look at a long pass launched by Brett before McHale was ready to recruit him.

Brett played for the Golden Eagles at Southern Mississippi, and quickly became a standout star. He was a natural leader on the field, and his teammates looked up to him. One of his best moments of leadership occurred during the 1989 season, when he led the team to a stunning, unexpected, last-minute victory. The Golden Eagles were facing off against the Seminoles from Florida State University—major rivals of Southern Mississippi.

This was a road game, with the Golden Eagles playing on the Seminoles' home turf in Jacksonville, Florida. The Seminoles had their best players on the field, and their fans were cheering them on. The game was intense, and by the last quarter, the Golden Eagles were stuck at 24 points, while their rivals maintained a two-point lead at 26.

Most people figured that the Golden Eagles were about to lose, but with just seconds left, Brett led a last-ditch drive down the field for a touchdown. The Golden Eagles were victorious, with a final score of 30 to 26, and Brett was now a bona fide hero at Mississippi.

Upon the team's arrival back to Hattiesburg, they were greeted by mobs of fans who wished to congratulate their new champion. Brett was their new Superman, but, just like the Man of Steel, who was vulnerable to Kryptonite, Brett wasn't without his own weaknesses. This was demonstrated when he nearly died in a car accident his senior year. The incident occurred on July 14, 1990. Brett was driving near his parents' house when, after being temporarily blinded by the bright lights of a passing car, he badly misjudged a turn. He swerved to the side, then overcorrected and lost control entirely, hitting an embankment.

Brett's Nissan Maxima flipped over and struck a tree before coming to a stop in a ruined, wrecked heap. The car looked terrible, and Brett was fortunate to have simply survived the ordeal. He was pulled out of the wreckage, rushed to the hospital, and had to have emergency surgery. As it turns out, the very thing that saved his life—his seatbelt—had also managed to injure him. The seatbelt had pressed into his stomach with such force that it had caused serious internal injuries. At first, it wasn't clear how serious they were. Doctors only mentioned that he had sustained lacerations to his liver and some pretty terrible bruising to his abdomen. Brett was told to take it easy so he could recover.

Shortly after leaving the hospital, however, he began to realize his injuries were a bit worse than he thought, especially when he discovered that he couldn't eat. When he attempted to swallow food, it came right back up. Football players have to eat to keep their strength up, but Brett was entirely unable to eat anything.

He was immediately taken back to the hospital, where the reason behind his inability to hold food down was discovered. Part of his intestine had been crushed during the accident, so food could no longer pass through his digestive system. The food was unable to exit his body normally, so he was vomiting everything back up shortly after consuming it. Needless to say, this had to be fixed.

Before it was all said and done, he ended up having 30 inches of his small intestine removed. It took him a while to recover after his surgery, but after several weeks off the field, Brett Favre made his return on September 8, 1990, just in time to secure a major win against Alabama. However, before he secured the win, there was a pretty scary moment on the field when Brett was sacked. He was knocked to the ground, and there was a hushed silence on the field as just about everyone feared that his intestines might have somehow been torn open. To everyone's relief, Brett was just a bit winded, and soon got right back up. He may have been knocked down, but he proved that he most certainly wasn't out! The Golden Eagles beat Alabama 27 to 24 that day, and the University of Southern Mississippi finished 8-3 for the season.

By the time his senior year came around, Brett Favre had generated quite a bit of interest from the NFL. Shortly after graduating from Southern Mississippi, he was picked up by the Atlanta Falcons in the 1991 NFL draft. He was picked in the second round, and was the 33rd overall pick.

The deal he made with the Atlanta Falcons was for a three-year contract worth $1.4 million. It was a good deal for Brett, but head coach Jerry Glanville was initially very skeptical of his new player. In fact, Brett was rarely let out onto the field, and the few times he was allowed to play, it didn't go too well.

After just one short season, Brett was traded to the Green Bay Packers in 1992. Green Bay's general manager Ron Wolf saw the promise in Brett and wanted him on the team. He recognized the potential of Brett's throwing arm, as well as his capacity for leadership on the field.

Brett Favre was 22 years old when he made his debut with the Packers in 1992, and to many, he was still a bit of an unknown. Even though Wolf saw his potential, there were still a lot of doubts about young quarterback.

Brett proved himself during the second game of his first season with the Packers. The Packers were playing against the Cincinnati Bengals, and the Bengals seemed poised to trounce the Packers. At the start of the game, Brett wasn't the starting quarterback. The team was instead using Don Majkowski. But Majkowski's magic didn't seem to be working, and Coach Mike Holmgren decided to give Brett a try. Brett's efforts on the field that day weren't perfect. In fact, he fumbled the ball on more than one occasion. Nevertheless, he was able to rally the team and began to put up scores for the Packers. It was a nail biter, but with just seconds left on the clock, Brett threw the game-winning pass.

Favre's last-minute victory set the Green Bay fans on fire. From that moment on, Brett Favre was their man. He became starting quarterback for the Packers and led the team on a six-game winning streak during the 1992 season. Brett was also named to the Pro Bowl for the first time—but certainly not the last.

Brett was NFL MVP in 1995, and in the 1996 season he took the team to the Super Bowl. It's an accomplishment just to make it to the Super Bowl, but could the Packers actually win it?

The Packers faced off against the New England Patriots. Green Bay drew first blood, and soon had a 10-0 lead.

But Drew Bledsoe and the New England Patriots weren't just going to sit down and take a beating. They clawed their way back on top, scoring two touchdowns to put them ahead 14 to 10. Then incredible 81-yard touchdown pass from Brett Favre to wide receiver Antonio Freeman put the Packers back in front, making the score 17 to 14. The Packers then managed to score a field goal, widening their lead over the Patriots to 20 to 14. The Packer's continued their run, and ended up winning Super Bowl XXXI 35 to 21.

The next year, Brett Favre and the Green Bay Packers returned to the championship game for Super Bowl XXXII, hoping for a repeat. It was an epic battle between the Packers and the Denver Broncos, with the teams trading scores for much of the game. The Broncos ultimately prevailed, however, beating the Packers 31 to 24.

Brett hit a slump in the late 1990s, but made a comeback in the early 2000s. He seemed to be hitting his peak when he received the sad news of his father's passing during the 2003 season, right before a crucial football game. Brett was devastated, as his dad meant everything to him.

Most people would have canceled everything that they were doing in order to grieve the loss, but not Brett Favre. On the contrary, he was determined to play the very next day, in honor of his dad, who had put so much faith in him and his career.

Brett's career began to wind down after his dad's passing, and many wondered if he was going to retire. He seemed to announce as much in 2008, when he held a press conference and stated that it was his intention to call it quits.

But he had a change of heart. Rather than retire, he simply switched teams. He played for the Jets in 2008, and then the Vikings from 2009 to 2010. Brett finally called it quits for good after the 2010 season.

FIVE FUN FACTS

- Brett Favre achieved three MVP awards in a row.
- Brett Favre threw over 70,000 career passing yards.
- He was the first quarterback to defeat all 32 NFL teams.
- Brett once claimed that he got his arm from his mother. Why? Because she once got mad and threw a pastrami sandwich at him. That sandwich apparently sailed through the air at incredible speed and hit Brett right in the head.
- In Kiln, Mississippi, Brett Favre's father Irvin has a street named after him—Irvin Favre Road.

SOME TRIVIA!

How many teams did Brett Favre play for in the NFL?

He played on four different teams: The Atlanta Falcons, the Green Bay Packers, the New York Jets, and the Minnesota Vikings.

How many Super Bowl rings does Brett Favre have?

He has one Super Bowl ring.

What movie did Bret Favre make a cameo appearance in?

In 1998, he had a small part in the film There's Something About Mary.

What high school did Brett Favre attend?

He went to Hancock North Central in Kiln, Mississippi.

Who is Brett Favre's favorite musical artist?

He is proud of his rural roots and likes the country music of Tim McGraw.

REAL-LIFE LESSONS

- Brett Favre listened to and respected his parents. If they gave him advice, he listened. That's a good quality for any young person to have.
- Brett had plenty of fun, but he also learned to value hard work. We should all develop this important trait.
- Brett Favre was a natural leader during intense, do-or-die moments on the football field. He knew how to delegate tasks and direct his teammates to execute game-winning drives. Being able to lead the way is a great skill for both football and life in general.
- Life is fragile. Brett Favre learned that the hard way when he crashed his car into an embankment and had to undergo emergency surgery. Handle life with care and don't take anything for granted.
- With tears still in his eyes, Brett Favre famously played a football game right after his dad passed. It wasn't easy, but Brett knew that his father would have preferred it that way.

BEN ROETHLISBERGER
BIG BEN AND THE ONE FOR THE THUMB

Ben Roethlisberger was born on March 2, 1982, in the small Midwestern town of Lima, Ohio. Ben didn't have it easy growing up, as his parents split up shortly after he was born. His father remarried, and Ben was primarily raised by his dad and stepmother. Sadly, Ben never really got to know his mother very well, since her life was cut short by a tragic car accident when Ben was eight years old.

Nevertheless, with the help of his father, Ben grew up to be a goal-oriented young man who looked forward to his future—and by high school, that future increasingly involved sports. Ben played football, baseball, and basketball in high school, but by his senior year, he began to focus mostly on football.

After graduating high school, he ended up going to Miami University on a full football scholarship to play for the Miami RedHawks. Those not familiar with Ohio and the colleges in the state can be forgiven for thinking that of South Florida when they hear the name Miami, because as it turns out, this school was not located near a beach. Instead, Miami University is in Oxford, Ohio!

Ben later picked up the nickname "Big Ben," but in his college days, the name "Big Slim" might have been more appropriate. He was certainly tall enough for football at 6 foot 5, but he was a bit on the skinny side. He hadn't yet picked up the bulk that he would become known for later in his career.

Ben was sidelined for much of his freshman season, but he practiced and worked on adding some bulk to his frame. The following year, he was made starting quarterback for the team. There was no stopping him after that. He put up impressive stats, and during his junior year, the Redhawks achieved a 13-1 record.

At this point, Ben was already good enough for the pros, and he made the decision not to return to school for his senior year. Instead, he made it known that he would be available for the 2004 NFL Draft. He was picked up by the Pittsburgh Steelers, who had been in search of a solid quarterback for some time and felt that Ben just might fit that bill.

Ben hit the ground running, with a 66.4 % completion rate his first season. The next year was also a good one for him, and he took the Steelers all the way to the Super Bowl. The big game took place on February 5th, 2006, and saw the Steelers facing off against the Seattle Seahawks.

Initially, the Seahawks seemed to be dominating, as they nailed a series of spectacular plays in the first quarter. Things changed by the second quarter, however, when Ben seemed to find his footing. The Steelers ended up winning with a final score of 21 to 10.

Considering the fact that the Steelers hadn't won a Super Bowl since the days of Terry Bradshaw, back in 1980, Ben seemed to be the answer that the Steelers had been looking for. Adding to the previous four Super Bowls the Steelers had won in the past, folks in Pittsburgh joked that this epic fifth Super Bowl ring was the "one for the thumb."

Unfortunately, the following season saw Ben Roethlisberger injured and sidelined much of the year. Interestingly enough, one of his injuries had absolutely nothing at all to do with football. Instead, on June 12, 2006, Ben was riding his motorcycle and crashed into a car at an intersection. Ben was tossed off the bike and slammed his head into the windshield of the car he had collided with. He should have been wearing a helmet, but he wasn't. Ben wore helmets on the football field, but he didn't realize they were just as important when riding a motorcycle!

Fortunately, there were enough quick-thinking witnesses there to get Ben to the hospital. He was rushed off to Pittsburgh's Mercy Hospital, where he was treated for a broken jaw, crushed sinus cavity, and nasty head wound from where he slammed into the windshield. Teammates and fans rallied around Ben and he made a speedy recovery.

He was still recovering when the Steelers opened up the season at Heinz Field on September 3, 2006. They did well enough without him, and backup quarterback Charlie Batch eked out a 28-17 win over the Miami Dolphins. But it was a real bummer to have the Steelers' Super Bowl champion quarterback sitting on the bench.

Fortunately, Ben got back in the huddle a short time later, but he was still trying to heal up his sore body. He was a little slower than normal, and the fact that opposing teams enjoyed sacking him didn't help matters much. He ended up losing three straight games—a devastating slump for a Super Bowl champ to find himself in.

Ben got back on track in 2007, and credited to his comeback to Coach Mike Tomlin. Tomlin had just been hired by the Steelers, and the 2007 season was his first with the team. Almost immediately, Mike and Ben seemed to forge a close bond with each other.

Football teams always seem to be at their best when the quarterback is in sync with the coach, and that season, the special relationship between these two seemed to be on full display. The first game of the year saw the Steelers run roughshod over the Cleveland Browns, beating them 34-7. Ben had a great season, and even though the team didn't make it to the Super Bowl, he made it to the Pro Bowl. Big Ben was back.

The 2008 season saw Ben and the Steelers in top form, and they once again made it to the Super Bowl. The Steelers appeared in Super Bowl XLIII on February 1, 2009, where they squared off against the Arizona Cardinals. Ben once again led the Steelers to victory with a 27-23 win. For a guy who's career was almost ended by a motorcycle accident, this was proof that he had fully recovered.

Ben's career ebbed and flowed after this second Super Bowl win. He had his ups and downs, including a Super Bowl defeat in 2010 at the hands of the Green Bay Packers. But he took it all in stride, putting in impressive performances on the field until his retirement in 2022.

FIVE FUN FACTS

- Ben played for Miami University in Ohio.
- He was the youngest quarterback to win a Super Bowl.
- He won two Super Bowls for the Pittsburgh Steelers.
- Ben got married to Ashley Harlan in 2011.
- His jersey for the Steelers was number 7.

SOME TRIVIA!

Where did Ben grow up?

He grew up in Findlay, Ohio.

Other than quarterback, what other positions has Ben played?

Back in his college days, he occasionally served as a punter and in high school, he once played as a wide receiver.

What player did Ben throw the game-winning touchdown pass to in Super Bowl XLIII?

Santonio Holmes.

What are some products that Roethlisberger has marketed with his name on them?

Big Ben's BBQ Sauce and Big Ben's XL Beef Jerky.

How many Pro Bowls did Ben appear in?

Ben appeared in six Pro Bowls.

REAL-LIFE LESSONS

- Never give up hope! The Steelers hadn't won a Super Bowl in decades, until Ben came around to win one for the thumb.
- Don't take unnecessary risks. Ben learned the hard way how an unnecessary risk, such as riding a motorcycle without a helmet, could jeopardize his football career—and quite possibly his life.

- Give credit where credit is due. Ben credited a lot of his later success with the Steelers to Coach Mike Tomlin. Don't hesitate to give praise to those who deserve credit.
- Be a team player. Ben didn't do it all on his own—he had excellent teammates helping him every step of the way.
- Never stop trying. Ben faced a slump after his first Super Bowl win, but he persevered and was able to win another one.

J.J. WATT
THE SWAT MACHINE

Fans know J.J. Watt as J.J. Swat, because of the way that he manages to swat balls out of the air. But when this future superstar was born on March 22, 1989, his actual given name was Justin James Watt. He didn't pick up the nickname J.J. until later in his childhood.

Born in Waukesha, Wisconsin, but raised primarily in Pewaukee, J.J. grew up playing all kinds of sports. It might surprise some of his fans to know that out of all of the sports that he played in his youth, football was not his favorite. He liked it well enough, but his true love was actually hockey.

Growing up in the cold north, hockey was a favorite pastime of many youngsters—J.J. included. The only trouble with hockey was the huge amount of time and money that it required. Hockey players have to fork out a lot of cash for all of their gear, and they also have to travel far from home a lot of the time. So, despite his love for the sport, J.J. started putting his energy elsewhere.

At the age of 13, J. J. stopped playing hockey and began to look more seriously at football. During his freshman year in high school in 2003, he managed to make the team at his school—the Pewaukee Pirates. He was tall for his age, but kind of skinny. His folks weren't worried, however, since all of the men of the family had filled out later in life.

J.J. was benched for the first couple of seasons with the team, but he soon found his time to shine. In 2005, the school took on a new coach—Clay Iverson—who decided to try J.J. as tight end. He had grown to a whopping 6 foot five, and by his senior year he weighed in at 235 pounds.

J.J. was no longer the skinny bean pole who had first tried out for the Pewaukee Pirates, and when he finished high school he was given a scholarship to Central Michigan University. Initially J.J. Watt played tight end at the college, but after catching just eight passes his entire first season, his coach decided to try him on the offensive line.

J.J. didn't want to play this position. Determined to take a different path, he decided to transfer to the University of Wisconsin. But the move came with a sacrifice. He didn't get to start at Wisconsin right away, and instead had to sit out the 2008 season. During this time, he took classes at a local community college and got a job delivering pizza for Pizza Hut.

It certainly wasn't a glamorous start for a future football star, but he did what he had to in order to achieve his dreams. And sure enough, after biding his time, he played his first game for Wisconsin in 2009. With his new team, he began to play as played as a defensive end and was a pivotal part of the team's formidable defense. In fact, during the 2010 season, he managed to finish number one in sacks for the team. He was so good that he didn't end up finishing college, instead accepting an offer from the NFL.

He was drafted in 2011 and had a promising first season with the Texans, who managed to reach the playoffs that year. One of his most memorable moments of the season occurred during an intense matchup with the Cincinnati Bengals. J.J. intercepted a pass from Andy Dalton and ran it back 29 yards to the end zone for a touchdown! It was unexpected, unilateral moves like this that eventually made J.J. famous.

As good as his debut season was, it was his second year on the team when he really proved his worth. During 2012, he averaged one sack a game, keeping the opposing quarterbacks on their toes. J.J. was like a human missile, launching himself at quarterbacks as soon as they tried to throw the ball.

J.J. didn't only have quarterbacks in his sights—he was more than ready to make life difficult for just about anyone on the opposing team. A great example was during an epic 2012 game against Indianapolis, when J.J. denied the Colts a chance to score at the one-yard line by knocking the ball right out of running back Mewelde Moore's hands! Some say it was a punch, while others say it was more akin to a judo chop. Whatever it was, J.J. struck with surgical precision and forced the fumble, which the Texans recovered. Crucial plays like this often turned into game-changers for his team.

In addition to turnovers, J.J. was known for his sacs. In 2014, he logged 20.5 of them! You might wonder how it's possible to earn half a sack. In football, it's considered half a sack when another defensive player is involved. If J.J. had one of his teammates helping him tackle the quarterback, they each earned half a sack.

Of course, J.J. never needed much in the way of assistance with his sacks. He was a full-blown sacking machine, all by himself. It's incredible how far he went with his NFL career, just a few years after delivering pizzas to people's homes. That just goes to show how important it is to persevere and never give up on your dreams. J.J. didn't give up, and neither should you!

FIVE FUN FACTS

- J.J.'s younger brother T.J. Watt plays for the Pittsburgh Steelers.
- J.J. has his own line of shoes and clothing.
- He is involved with several charitable organizations.
- J.J. is a gifted orator and engages in motivational speaking.
- In 2017, J.J. was named Sports Illustrated Sportsperson of the Year.

SOME TRIVIA!

What feat did J.J. repeat in both 2012 and 2013?

In both of these seasons, he achieved more than 20 sacks.

How many Super Bowl rings does J.J. Watt have?

As good as he was, he doesn't have any. His team never appeared in the Super Bowl.

Does he have a nickname?

Yes, he's called J.J. Swat because of the way he can swat balls right out of the air.

What TV show has he appeared on?

He made a cameo appearance on an episode of New Girl.

What did J.J. raise $41 million for in 2017?

To aid the relief efforts for those who were hit by Hurricane Harvey in and around Houston, Texas.

REAL-LIFE LESSONS

- Things didn't quite work out for J.J. at Central Michigan University, so he decided to transfer to the University of

Wisconsin. We all have to make important decisions about what's best for us in life.

- J.J. couldn't enroll at the University of Wisconsin right away, so he took classes at a community college and delivered pizza instead. It wasn't the most glamorous part of his story, but sometimes you just have to do the best you can in life in order to advance to the next chapter.

- J.J. wanted to play as a defensive end for Wisconsin, and did what he could to demonstrate his abilities on the field. His dedication paid off, and he became an invaluable member of the team.

- J.J. never hesitated to take initiative. Without being told to do anything, he would make major moves on the field, and at times even take the ball into his own hands to score a touchdown on his own. We should all learn to take the initiative in life, just as he did.

- Above all else, J.J. learned to persevere in both football and in life. Remember that perseverance is key to anything that you do.

BAKER MAYFIELD
THE BAKER'S DOZEN

Football star Baker Mayfield was born to James and Gina Mayfield on April 14, 1995. Football was in his blood, since his father James was a star quarterback and punter during his college years at the University of Houston.

Growing up, it seemed a given that little Baker would play football. When he was a kid, there were three things that commanded his attention the most—football, baseball, and video games. At first, baseball took up the vast majority of his time. He played on Little League teams as a youngster, and was a first baseman for Lake Travis High School, where he managed to earn Class 4A all-state honors. Those who knew him predicted that he might someday go pro, but fate had other things in store for Baker Mayfield.

As it turns out, his biggest problem when it came to football was his size. Baker is still small for a quarterback, even today, but back when he was in high school he was even smaller. His small stature might have seemed ideal for baseball, but it raised some doubts when it came to football.

Mayfield later recalled that he stood 5 foot 2 and weighed around 130 pounds during his freshman year of high school. Most of the kids were already much bigger than him, and it took him a while to catch up. He eventually did, however, and was soon taking football at Lake Travis High School to new heights. He became the team's starting quarterback and won the 2011 4A state championship.

After graduating from high school in 2012, Baker enrolled at Texas Tech. This wasn't his first choice, but many other schools had overlooked him due to his size. He had gotten a bit bigger by this time, but his hands were still small. As funny as that might sound, scouts took one look at his hands and thought that he might have trouble catching and throwing the ball.

This was a snap judgment that they would come to regret. After Texas Tech gave him a chance and made him starting quarterback, Baker took the football field by storm during the 2013 season. He was filling in for the previous starter, Michael Brewer, who had been sidelined by an injury. Baker realized that all eyes were on him, and he was determined not to let anyone down.

That first season he threw 12 touchdown passes and was named the "best freshman offensive player in his conference." Despite all of these accolades, he found that his coach rubbed him the wrong way. As anyone who understands football knows, the relationship between a coach and quarterback is crucial. If they are not in sync, the entire team can suffer.

Baker tried to connect with his coach on a personal level, but it just didn't work. As a result, after his first season with Texas Tech, he decided to cut his losses and switch gears. He signed with the University of Oklahoma, where he kicked off an explosive season in 2015.

This was a great year for Baker Mayfield, but it wasn't without its share of hardship. The hardest thing that Baker faced in 2015 was when his mother, Gina, was in a terrible car accident. She and Baker's Aunt Kristi Brooks were being driven by their friend Adrienne Davis when the accident happened. Adrienne was killed in the crash, while the other two women survived. Gina's seatbelt saved her from dying, but also pressed into her stomach, causing an injury. It took her a while to recover, but fortunately she survived.

Baker excelled at the University of Oklahoma, averaging 40 touchdown passes a season. He also won the 2017 Heisman Trophy, which is an annual award handed out to the most promising player in college football for that particular season.

In 2018, he was drafted by the Cleveland Browns. He got straight down to business with the Browns, where he was known as a hard worker from the beginning. His daily routine consisted of getting up early, having a cup of coffee, taking a shower, eating a light breakfast, and then working out. In the gym, he would do several sets of pushups, pull ups, and other exercises. Baker would often switch up his exercise routine to simulate the randomness of the moves he had to make on the football field. For instance, he's been known to do pushups, then suddenly jump to his feet, grab an exercise ball, hurl it across the room, and then run like his life depends on it. He knows that all of these activities—as funny as they may seem—are important for keeping him in shape for when he steps onto the field. The Cleveland Browns had a bad rep as an underperforming organization and needed someone dedicated like Baker.

Baker proved that he was more than up for the challenge. With his help, soon the Browns were not just winning games, but dominating the field. However, they still ended the 2019 season with a rather lackluster 6-10 record. Improvements had been made, but there was still much work to be done.

Baker began the 2020 season more hopeful, especially after a week two win against the Cincinnati Bengals, whom the Browns beat in a nail biter, 35-30 victory. Unfortunately, much of the 2020 season was affected by the COVID-19 pandemic. Baker was also sidelined for part of the season when he contracted COVID-19. He eventually recovered, and the Browns finished the 2020 season 11-5.

The 2021 season was not Baker's best, and he ended up getting traded to the Carolina Panthers. He started playing for the Panthers during the 2022 season. However, halfway through the year, he was traded to the Los Angeles Rams. He was then traded once again to the Tampa Bay Buccaneers, with whom he signed on March 16, 2023. His stats with the Buccaneers have been mixed, but he is currently still playing with the team. Baker might be a work in progress, but so are we all!

FIVE FUN FACTS

- Baker Mayfield won the Heisman Trophy in 2017.
- He has an active social media presence.
- Baker is a big fan of music and has a large record collection.
- He loves animals, and is known for being out and about with his dogs.
- He's known as both a team leader and a perfectionist.

SOME TRIVIA!

Does he have a hobby?

He loves video games—especially *Halo*.

How many teams has Baker Mayfield played for so far in his career?

As of this writing, Mayfield has played for three teams—the Cleveland Browns, the Los Angeles Rams, and the Tampa Bay Buccaneers.

How many Super Bowl Rings does Baker Mayfield have?

So far, he has none.

What insurance company has Baker Mayfield advertised for?

He's appeared in commercials for Progressive Insurance.

What other sports does he enjoy?

Baker Mayfield plays golf.

REAL-LIFE LESSONS

- During his early days playing football, it was common for others to underestimate Baker due to his small size. Baker learned not to let such things discourage him. He didn't let all of the snap judgments and narrowminded opinions of others diminish his own sense of self-worth. This is a good lesson for all of us to learn.

- Baker learned how crucial the relationship is between a player and coach. He realized that he wasn't connecting well with his coach at Texas Tech, and made the choice to switch to the University of Oklahoma. We need to try our best in all of our relationships, but, like Baker learned, there are times when we need to just cut our losses and try something new.

- After his mom's bad car accident, Baker learned just how precious (and short) life is. This is a lesson we will all learn as we progress through our lives.

- Baker Mayfield knows the value of setting a good daily routine. He wakes up, drinks coffee, takes a shower, eats a light breakfast, and works out on a daily basis. It's good to have a solid, daily regimen to follow.

- Baker Mayfield saw a great (but achievable) challenge in improving the ranking of the Cleveland Browns. He knew it wasn't going to be easy, but he was more than ready to give it his best.

I have included these free downloadable gifts to help light up your inner inspiration & reach your potential.

While you are reading through the stories, lessons and trivia, we recommend that you make use of all the bonuses we've attached here!

All our bonuses have been made specifically to help young athletes feel fired up, get inspired from the best to ever do it, and most importantly fall more in love with this incredible game!

Here's a list of what you're getting:

1) 250 Fun Facts From The World Of Sports
2) Sports Practice and Game Calendar
3) 5 Fun Exercise Drills for Kids
4) The BEST Advice From The Greatest Athletes Of All Time
5) The Mental Mindset Guided Meditation & Affirmation Collection
6) The Most Famous Events In Sports History And What They Can Teach Us

Now, it's over to you to scan the QR code, follow the instructions & get started!

DREW BREES
THE COMEBACK KID

Born in Dallas, Texas, on January 15, 1979, Drew Brees came from a family of athletes. Mina and Chip, Drew's mother and father, were lawyers by trade but athletes by choice. Chip had played basketball at Texas A&M University, while Mina had been an all-star tennis player back in high school. They encouraged athleticism in their kids, and Drew and his little brother Reid grew up to be avid football and baseball players.

Sadly, Drew's parents split up in 1987, and Drew and his brother Reid spent the rest of their childhood being shuffled back and forth between their two parents, who maintained shared custody of them. During the summer, they also spent time with Mina's dad, Grandpa Ray.

Drew's grandfather was a football star in his day, and was remembered for tearing up the field at Southwest Texas State College. After he graduated, he served as a high school football coach for 38 years. During that time, Drew and his brother Reid often showed up at the school their grandpa coached—Gregory Portland High—to watch games.

Along with his love for all things football, Drew also picked up his mother's passion for tennis. He actually played competitive tennis until the age of 13. Many have long wondered if his agility as a quarterback, and especially his ability to quickly hop around on his feet, might have something to do with those early years on the tennis court.

In 1993, Drew began his freshman year at Westlake High School. He was the school's starting quarterback by his sophomore year. The player who was meant to be the starter injured his knee, opening the door for Drew to be the team's leader.

Drew showed what he could do on the field, and remained the starter for the rest of his high school career. In 1996, he led Westlake to the state championship. His old high school coach, Neal LaHue, later sang Drew's praises. He recalled Drew having great leadership qualities, a strong work ethic, and a good attitude. Drew was the most responsible, respectful, and just plain nice kid that Coach LaHue ever taught. These were all traits that Drew continued to display to friends, family, and teammates alike.

Upon graduating high school, Drew was hoping to play for his dad's old collegiate team, Texas A&M. But after failing to generate interest there, he ended up attending Purdue University in Indiana. Purdue is known for its engineering program, and Drew ended up majoring in industrial management.

During his time at Purdue, he became an active member of Sigma Chi fraternity. But Drew was primarily at Purdue to play football, and the school did not disappoint in this department. Purdue is home to the famed Purdue Boilermakers, and at the time of Drew's arrival, Coach Joe Tiller was developing a unique coaching strategy referred to as "basketball on grass," due to the way that he spread out the offensive positions of his players on the field.

Drew was initially the backup quarterback, and during that first season he didn't get a lot of time on the field. But he made up for his inaction during games by committing to tremendous outreach outside of them. He took part in the Gentle Giants initiative, which had football players make trips to local elementary schools to help disadvantaged students. The football players were meant to be helpful, gentle giants to these youngsters, and Drew most certainly fit that bill. He was a mentor to many kids at Miller Elementary in Lafayette, and the school's second grade teacher, Jennifer Dickensheets, long remembered just how crucial his mentoring was. Along with visiting schools, Drew also worked with the Boys & Girls Club, the March of Dimes, and the Muscular Dystrophy Association.

When Drew was finally made starting quarterback for the Boilermakers, he took the role seriously. His hard work paid off, and by October he was setting records in both passing yards and touchdown passes. For the 1998 season, he was named the Big Ten's Offensive Player of the Year.

During the 1999 season, he was given the Socrates Award for extraordinary efforts in athletics and academics, as well as his community service efforts. However, the Boilermakers didn't do so well that season, finishing the year 7-5.

In 2000, Drew was being actively prospected for the NFL. However, he decided to finish his schooling, and led the Boilermakers to some great wins. That season, Drew threw 26 touchdown passes and Purdue finished with a 8-3 record. Drew was also a finalist for the prestigious Heisman trophy. He ended up finishing in third place.

Drew was drafted into the NFL by the San Diego Chargers in 2001. Other teams were hesitant because of Drew's height, preferring a quarterback who was at least six feet tall. Drew was a backup QB for the team, and he was once again looking for his chance to get out on the field so that he could prove his worth. That chance finally came during the 2002 season, when Drew was made starting quarterback.

Chargers did better than they had during their lackluster 2001 season, and with Drew leading the team they finished with a record of 8-8. The following year, they did even better. That was also the year Drew married his college sweetheart, Brittany Dudchenko.

Drew started the 2004 season with renewed determination. The Chargers had some difficulty in the first few weeks, but by week four, Drew was dominating. He had 16 completions, three touchdowns, and zero interceptions, helping the Chargers trounce the Tennessee Titans, 38-17. This was followed by a victory against the Jacksonville Jaguars, 34-21. The Chargers then lost to the Atlanta Falcons, 21-20, but it was a nail-biter that displayed everything that was great about Drew Brees.

This loss was followed by an eight-game winning streak that saw San Diego end the stunning season with a 12-4 record. Drew emerged from the 2004 season as one of the most promising quarterbacks in the NFL.

The 2005 season was also a good one for Drew, although the overall team record dipped to 9-7. Unfortunately, tragedy struck in the final game of the season. The Chargers were playing against the Broncos, and there was a lot of pressure on Drew. He was attempting to make a pass when John Lynch, a safety for the Broncos, slammed into him, causing him to fumble the football. Drew was attempting to recover the ball when a huge defensive tackle named Gerald Warren came crashing down right on top of Drew's arm.

It was as if a mountain had just fallen on top of him, and the immense weight dislocated Drew's shoulder. It was a bad injury, and Drew ended up having to get surgery. He eventually recovered, but decided not to stay with the San Diego Chargers for another season. Contract talks had broken down, and Brees decided he wasn't getting paid enough in San Diego.

Drew later admitted that he was worried the team was giving up on him due to his injury. He had always been a very sensitive person, and he felt that he was being given subtle cues by management that they were distancing themselves from him. So rather than being slowly phased out, Drew decided to go elsewhere, where his talents might be better appreciated.

The two teams that showed interest in him were the Miami Dolphins and the New Orleans Saints. The Saints offered Drew a $19 million guaranteed payout for his first year, along with a $12 million option for the second, and he accepted the offer.

Drew's first year with the Saints was a good one. But there was a lot going on outside of the football stadium, as well. The previous year, in the fall of 2005, New Orleans had been hit by Hurricane Katrina. As the new quarterback for the New Orleans Saints, Drew made it his mission not just to be a good player on the field, but also a good person off of it.

Drew quickly got involved in community work. He had already established "The Brees Dream Foundation" back in 2003, to raise money for good causes such as cancer research and aid for disadvantaged kids, and he immediately turned the focus of his foundation on New Orleans and the efforts of getting the city back on its feet after Katrina. He not only raised money and awareness for good causes, but also made sure that he had a presence in the community and let people know that he cared about them. Drew frequented restaurants, local stores, parks, and other attractions, making himself a common fixture of New Orleans.

Building on this platform of goodwill, Drew launched into the 2006 season for the New Orleans Saints. He was fully recovered from his injury and was consistent as a pass thrower and play caller. The biggest moment of the season came during week three, when the Saints made their return to the Louisiana

Superdome. The team had not played on its home turf since Katrina, as the Superdome had been converted into an emergency shelter for New Orleans residents. But in week three of the 2006 season, the Superdome was finally cleared to once again serve its original purpose as a football stadium.

This was a big moment for New Orleans residents, to see their football stadium returned to normal and their home team back in business. The was treated as a kind of celebration—a Mardi Gras-style event, with bands giving concerts and open barbecues taking place for fans. But once the game commenced, all eyes were on Drew Brees and the Saints as they took on the Atlanta Falcons. Would this new quarterback live up to all of the hype?

The New Orleans fans were not disappointed, as the Saints trounced the Falcons in a blowout victory, 23-3. Drew Brees proved that he had recovered from his terrible injury, and the whole city of New Orleans proved that they had made a comeback of their own.

Drew learned an important lesson that day—that we can grow stronger in the face of adversity. He took this philosophy with him all the way to the Super Bowl in 2010, where he led the Saints to a stunning 46-34 victory over the Indianapolis Colts. Drew then played several more great seasons with the Saints before retiring in 2021.

FIVE FUN FACTS

- Drew played in the NFL for 20 seasons.
- He was a football star at Westlake High School, and led his team to a 16-0 record.
- Drew Brees graduated from Purdue in 2001.
- He began his NFL career as a backup quarterback for Doug Flutie.
- His first professional NFL game was against the Kansas City Chiefs.

SOME TRIVIA!

Where was Drew Brees born?

He was born in Dallas, Texas.

How many times has Drew Brees appeared in the Pro Bowl?

He's appeared 13 times.

For what NFL teams did Drew Brees play?

He played for the San Diego Chargers before switching to the New Orleans Saints.

How many Super Bowl rings does he have?

Drew has one.

What is his favorite food?

He's been known to enjoy deep Southern cuisine. Drew is most especially fond of the New Orleans favorite—a country-fried steak po-boy sandwich.

When did Drew Brees retire?

He retired in 2021.

REAL-LIFE LESSONS

- Drew Brees was an avid sports fan at a young age, and enjoyed playing sports of all kinds. He was tearing up the tennis court at just 13 years of age. Many believe that his diverse athletic background contributed to his incredible talent on the football field. Drew learned early on that variety is the spice of life. Don't limit yourself! To be successful in football and in life, you should experiment with a wide variety of fields and subjects.

- Ever since he was a kid, Drew was known to be polite, respectful, and a hard worker. These are all great qualities to have. These qualities convinced many people that Drew had what it took to be a great leader, both on and off the football field.

- Drew originally had his heart set on going to Texas A&M, but when that didn't work out, he quickly adjusted his plans and set his sights on Purdue, instead. Don't get discouraged if your first choice doesn't work out. Like Drew, you've just got to learn to roll with the punches.

- Drew Brees was an excellent mentor for young people. He engaged in mentoring back in his Purdue days, when he took part in the Gentle Giants program. He learned how satisfying it is to be able to reach out and encourage others to succeed.

- By recovering from a terrible injury and restarting his career in the hurricane-ravaged city of New Orleans, Drew Brees learned the power of overcoming adversity. He realized that we can learn from hardship, and that whatever temporarily knocks us down only makes us stronger in the long run.

PATRICK MAHOMES
GIVING IT HIS ALL

Patrick Mahomes is one of the most unique and exciting players to grace the football field in recent times. He is an unconventional quarterback, and he uses his unorthodox methods to great advantage. He can throw with either arm if necessary—and there are even times when he can throw without looking where the ball is going. He throws longways, sideways, and along all the byways, but one thing is certain: His throws almost always connect.

Patrick was born in the hot and humid confines of Tyler, Texas, on September 17, 1995. He was the son of MLB baseball star Pat Mahomes and a Texas woman named Randi Martin. Patrick's parents didn't actually get married until 1998, when Patrick was three years old. It's unclear if Patrick remembers much of this event, but he was actually the ring bearer at his parents' wedding.

Patrick's father was a Major League pitcher for the New York Mets, and during the boy's childhood, he often traveled to watch his father play. As exciting and fun as all of this was, these good times ended in 2006, when his mother and father's marriage fell apart. Patrick spent the rest of his formative years in Whitehouse, Texas, with his mother, which was where he developed a love for both baseball and football.

Interestingly, Patrick later suggested that it was his training as a pitcher that helped him develop a lot of his unique football throws. Just imagine Patrick pitching curveballs on a baseball diamond, and then throwing his signature sidewinders on the football field, and you get an idea of how this might have come about.

Whitehouse High School was where Patrick first became a football star. He was good enough to be recruited by Texas Tech University and play on their college team. He began the 2014 season at Texas Tech as a backup quarterback for the team's starter, Davis Webb. But during a game against Oklahoma State, Patrick filled in for an injured Webb and was able to show the world what he was capable of.

He was given a few more opportunities that year, and managed to prove his worth each time. By his sophomore year, he was made the official starter for the team. That season, Patrick led the Big 12 Conference. He had 364 pass completions (out of 573 attempts), 36 touchdowns, and only 15 interceptions.

Off the field, Patrick was a marketing major who took his studies seriously. In fact, his grade point average was 3.71!

Patrick Mahome's later indicated that he had a near photographic memory. This skill was helpful when studying for tests, but it was also beneficial on the football field, where he had to memorize plays.

Patrick was ultimately drafted into the NFL in 2017. He had gained the interest of a few teams, most notably the Arizona Cardinals, Buffalo Bills, and Kansas City Chiefs. The Chiefs ultimately took the initiative and made Patrick a part of their team. He kept a low profile during the 2017 season, playing as a backup for starter Alex Smith. But once given a chance, he demonstrated his incredible ability to throw amazing passes, even when he was under tremendous pressure from the opposing team's defense. Former starter Alex Smith was subsequently traded, and Patrick Mahomes was given the position of starting quarterback.

As a starter, Patrick took the football world by storm. There were times when the Chiefs seemed almost unstoppable. But Patrick Mahomes and the Chiefs ran into a formidable roadblock toward the end of their winning season when they faced off against the New England Patriots. This dynamic team was still being led by veteran superstar Tom Brady and had a roster full of dynamic players. The Chiefs lost to the Patriots, but even with the loss, it was clear that Patrick Mahomes was a rising star in the game.

Patrick finished that season with 5,381 passing yards, 50 passing touchdowns, a 65.9 completion percentage, and an overall quarterback rating of 111.7. He then came back even stronger during the 2019 season and led his teammates to the Super Bowl. Super Bowl LIV took place on February 2, 2020, and marked the first time that the Chiefs had been to the championship game since 1970. Patrick and the Chiefs dominated the game, securing a Super Bowl win for the franchise after a 50-year drought. Patrick was named Super Bowl MVP for his efforts.

The Chiefs were hoping for a repeat in the 2020 season, and on February 7, 2021, made it to Super Bowl LV. This time, Patrick was playing against his old rival Tom Brady, who was now with the Tampa Bay Buccaneers. Brady played incredibly for the Tampa Bay Buccaneers, just as he had so many times for the Patriots, and the Chiefs ended up losing 39-9. The loss was disappointing, but Patrick Mahomes didn't let it get him down— he just tried harder. In fact, he ended up winning two more Super Bowls, back to back, in 2023 and 2024!

FIVE FUN FACTS

- Patrick Mahomes is also a gifted baseball player.
- He once threw a "no hitter" as a pitcher in high school.
- He was a standout star at Texas Tech, with a 63.5 completion rate.
- He won the Sammy Baugh Trophy during his junior year at Texas Tech.
- He's won back-to-back Super Bowls with the Kansas City Chiefs.

SOME TRIVIA!

What seasoning does Mahomes put on just about any food?

Ketchup. He loves it!

How many Super Bowl rings does Mahomes have?

He has three Super Bowl rings.

Does he have a nickname?

His dad called him "Showtime."

What commercials has he appeared in?

Patrick has done commercials for State Farm, Head & Shoulders, and Oakley.

Patrick Mahomes was the victim of what crime in 2017?

Patrick had just dropped off his girlfriend when he was waylaid by an assailant and robbed at gunpoint. He had his wallet stolen, but wasn't hurt. The robber was later arrested.

REAL-LIFE LESSONS

- Patrick Mahomes developed some rather unique techniques as a quarterback. He was willing to take skills learned as a pitcher on a baseball diamond and apply them to football. He learned the value of finding creative solutions to problems both on and off the football field.

- During his time at Texas Tech, Patrick Mahomes valued his academic education just as much as his athletic performance. He maintained a high grade point average and graduated with honors. He understood the importance of being a well-rounded individual. You can do well in everything that you put your mind to.

- At the start of his first season in the NFL, as a backup quarterback, Patrick Mahomes initially didn't see a whole lot of action. Nevertheless, he was always prepared. His preparation paid off when he was finally given the chance to take over as QB and demonstrate just how talented he was. Patrick learned the value of patience—something we should all learn.

- Patrick Mahomes learned to see the big picture. After a particularly rough season or a setback in the playoffs, he didn't dwell on mistakes. Instead, he focused on all of the ways he could improve as a player.

- After losing Super Bowl LV to the Tampa Bay Buccaneers, Patrick dedicated himself to trying even harder. He later won back-to-back Super Bowls as a result. We should all learn to develop a similar sense of dedication and determination.

TRAVIS KELCE
THE KELCE BOWL AWAITS

Travis Kelce—yet another explosive athlete who plays for the Kansas City Chiefs—was born on October 5, 1989. He began life in the town of Westlake, Ohio. His dad, Ed, worked in marketing, for an industrial firm. His mom, Donna, was a high-powered banking executive.

Travis had an older brother, Jason who has also become an NFL superstar. Both brothers would grow up in Westlake, Ohio, a suburb of Cleveland. Here their sibling rivalry and competitive drive was on full display for all to see. It was here that Travis attended Cleveland Heights High, and made a name for himself in both football, as well as baseball and basketball.

It was in football where he really stood out. During his senior year, in 2007, Travis gained All-Lake Erie League honors. After graduating from high school, he attended school at the University of Cincinnati on a football scholarship, playing for the Bearcats—a team that his brother, Jason, was already playing for.

Travis was a good player, but he got into trouble in 2010 when he tested positive for marijuana, and was subsequently suspended. He was back on the team for the 2011 season, and played tight end. The following season (2012) turned out to be one of his best, with high stats for receptions (45), receiving yards (722), and touchdowns (8). Travis Kelce also managed to earn first team all-conference honors.

Travis Kelce was drafted by the Kansas City Chiefs at the start of the 2013 season. He injured his knee before the official season actually started, however, and was benched for much of the year. The next season brought further challenges. He was sidelined numerous times, and at one point had to pay a hefty fine for unsportsmanlike conduct after an inappropriate hand gesture to Von Miller, a linebacker for the Denver Broncos.

Travis had gotten off to a rough start, but in the third game of the season he caught his first touchdown pass. After that, he made steady progress.

The following season proved to be better for the Chiefs, and for Travis Kelce, in particular, as he scored several touchdowns. Then, a few years later, in 2018, the Kansas City Chiefs decided to use Patrick Mahomes as their starting quarterback. That year, the combination of Travis Kelce and Patrick Mahomes blew the football world away.

The team made it to the playoffs in 2018, and the next year they made it all the way to the Super Bowl, where they ended up winning. Travis and Patrick led the Chiefs to victory over the San Francisco 49ers, with a final score of 31-20.

The next season, they once again made it to the Super Bowl, but came up short against Tom Brady and the Tampa Bay Buccaneers.

The Kelcey/Mahomes show wasn't over, though, as the Chiefs ultimately won two more back-to-back Super Bowls in 2023 and 2024. The 2023 Super Bowl win was perhaps the most memorable for Travis Kelce, since the Chiefs faced off against the Philadelphia Eagles—the team that Travis Kelce's brother Jason played for. The fact that the two brothers were facing off against each other had many people joking that this should be called the Kelce Bowl.

In 2024, the Chiefs once again took on the San Francisco 49ers in the Super Bowl. This time around, the score was much closer than it had been back in 2020. The Chiefs barely eked out a win in a game that had gone into overtime, with a final score of 25-22.

Interestingly, this game gained extra attention by way of Travis Kelce's romantic relationship with pop superstar Taylor Swift. The two had been dating for the past year, and there was so much media hype around this high-profile relationship that some dubbed the game the "Swiftie Bowl" in Taylor Swift's honor.

Unfortunately, Travis let his temper get the better of him during the game, and at one point screamed in the face of his coach, Andy Reid. Coach Reid remained stoic and calm during this incident, which made Travis's angry outburst seem even worse. He ultimately realized he had been a jerk, and later apologized for the incident. Travis learned an important lesson that day—that there is a fine line between passion and belligerence.

FIVE FUN FACTS

- Travis grew up in the suburbs of Ohio.
- He played college football for the Bearcats at the University of Cincinnati.
- Travis is now considered one of the best tight ends in the NFL.
- Travis Kelce has racked up seven consecutive seasons with 1,000 or more receiving yards.
- He maintains the record for most receptions by a tight end for his first 10 seasons.

SOME TRIVIA!

In what state was Kelce born?

He was born in Ohio.

What mayor did Kelce once talk smack to?

Travis is known to be feisty, and often doesn't hold back—even when it comes to mayors of major metropolitan cities. Just prior to an AFC championship game in January 2023, Cincinnati Mayor Aftab Pureval referred to the Chiwef's Arrowhead Stadium as "Burrowhead" in an apparent dig at the Chiefs. After the Chiefs beat the Bengals 23-20, ensuring that it would be the Chiefs who moved forward to the Super Bowl and not the Bengals, Kelce mocked Mayor Pureval's previous remarks by shouting out to a camera crew on the field, "Burrowhead my ass—it's Mahomes' house!"

In what Super Bowl did Travis Kelce face off against his brother, Jason Kelce?

Otherwise known as the "Kelce Bowl," Super Bowl LVII took place on February 12, 2023.

Did Travis Kelce appear in a reality TV show?

Yes, he appeared in the program "Catching Kelce," which focused on his dating life.

Who is Travis Kelce's famous girlfriend?

Even folks who don't like football know this one—he's dating music idol Taylor Swift.

REAL-LIFE LESSONS

- Travis Kelce learned the value of sportsmanship after his rather unsportsmanlike conduct ended up costing him a hefty fine. We all need to treat each other with respect and decency, both on and off the football field.

- Travis got off to a rough start during the 2014 season, but he kept his head down and continued to make noteworthy plays. He learned to tune out some of the noise around him and focus on simply doing a good job.

- After Patrick Mahomes became the official starter for the Chiefs in 2018, Travis Kelce learned the value of a winning combination. He was good before, but once he teamed up with Patrick, this dynamic duo became almost unstoppable. Both in football and in life, a solid, stable partnership can really do wonders.

- After his outburst against his coach went viral, Travis Kelce learned that there is a fine line between passion and belligerence. He's since promised to show better self-control. This is a lesson we should all take note of.

- The Kansas City Chiefs had to fight hard for their 2024 Super Bowl victory. They struggled all the way into overtime, where they eked out a victory. It wasn't easy, but a win is a win. Likewise, in the journey of life, we shouldn't worry so much about the minor details, but rather learn to enjoy the final destination.

GROWING UP AS JOE BURROW

The Cincinnati Bengals have had a bum rap as an underperforming football team for quite some time. Having that said, Joe Burrow just might be the best quarterback that ever played for the team.

Joe Burrow was born on December 10, 1996, to Jim and Robin Burrow. His dad was a football star in his youth, and later in life enjoyed a coaching gig at Iowa State University. He then moved to the University of Nebraska, and then North Dakota State University. Ultimately, he ended up as a defensive coordinator at Ohio University, relocating the family to Athens, Ohio.

In the meantime, young Joe Burrow managed to catch the football bug. He played as a quarterback and defensive lineman at Athens High School, where he was so calm under pressure that he was given the nickname "Joe Cool."

Joe Burrow graduated from high school in 2015, after spending his last three seasons on the school's varsity team. During his years at Athens High, he threw 157 touchdown passes and only 17 interceptions. After graduating, he had several colleges approach him, but he was determined to go to Ohio State University.

During his first two seasons at Ohio State, Joe served as a backup quarterback for J.T. Barrett. But he eventually got tired of being a backup and decided to try his luck elsewhere. He transferred to Louisiana State University in May of 2018, where he served as the starting quarterback for the LSU Tigers, helping them achieve a 10-3 record.

His 2019 season was even more memorable, especially because of a game that he played against LSU rivals Georgia Southern. LSU beat Georgia to smithereens, 55-3, with Joe scoring five touchdowns!

The next year, the team made it to the college playoffs, and actually finished with a perfect season—15-0. Joe was awarded the coveted Heisman Trophy for his efforts.

That year, the NFL came calling. Ironically, after completing a perfect season with his college team, Joe was drafted by a team in a deep slump—the Cincinnati Bengals. Once the regular season began, Joe was determined to turn around the Bengals previous slump. He started out promisingly enough, beating the Jacksonville Jaguars in the season opener. Unfortunately, Joe and his Bengals ended up losing four straight games after that.

The season ended even worse, as Joe suffered an injury. On November 22, 2020, he was hit so hard in the legs that his knee was knocked out of alignment, taking him out for the rest of the season. It was so bad that some people wondered if his career was over. Fortunately, after surgery and rehab, Joe Burrow bounced back.

Joe was in perfect form in the fall of 2021, when he led the Bengals to the top of the AFC North. In the process, the team stunned football fans by beating the reigning Super Bowl champs, the Kansas City Chiefs. This was a great confidence booster for the Bengals.

During this season, Burrow led the league in completions, with a 70.4% completion rate. Even better, he led the Bengals to the Super Bowl—something that many people thought was impossible only a few months before. The Bengals had not been to the Super Bowl since 1988.

While the Bengals lost to the Rams, 23 to 20, this was the best season they'd had in decades. They followed that up by making it to the playoffs again in the 2022/2023 season, but this time ended up losing to the rampaging Kansas City Chiefs. The Chiefs went on to win the Super Bowl that year.

The Cincinnati Bengals suffered some bad injuries during the following season, and Joe was benched much of the time. But if recent history has made anything clear, it is that you can't count Joe Burrows and the Bengals out, no matter what happens.

FIVE FUN FACTS

- Joe Burrow was born on December 10, 1996.
- He won the Heisman Trophy in 2019.
- He was picked by the Cincinnati Bengals in the 2020 NFL draft.
- Burrow is known as a natural leader on the field.
- Burrow and the Bengals came within striking distance of the Super Bowl in 2023, but were knocked out of the running by the Kansas City Chiefs.

SOME TRIVIA!

Does he have a nickname?

Due to his calm composure, he's been called "Joe Cool."

What NFL team did Joe's father Jim play for?

Jim Burrow played one season for the Green Bay Packers in 1976.

What major grocery store chain does Joe's girlfriend work for?

Joe Burrow's girlfriend, Olivia Holzmacher, works as a senior process specialist for grocery store juggernaut Kroger.

What's Joe Burrow's favorite TV show?

He's a fan of the cartoon SpongeBob SquarePants.

Who is Joe Burrow's famous musician friend?

Joe is good friends with rapper Kid Cudi.

REAL-LIFE LESSONS

- Joe Burrow is known to be cool under pressure, earning him the nickname "Joe Cool." He learned a long time ago that there is no sense in stressing out over the things you can't control. Just worry about the things you can improve upon, and don't sweat the rest.

- Joe Burrow learned to take things into his own hands. At Ohio State, he was tired of being stuck behind starter J.T. Barrett, so he decided to transfer to LSU. There are times in football, and in life, when we need to take the first step toward what we want.

- During his live-streamed NFL draft, in which millions of viewers tuned in to watch, Joe knew that all eyes were on him. He realized that he had to carry himself in a respectful and dignified manner. Most of us don't have as big of a following, but we should still follow Joe Burrow's classy example and carry ourselves well.

- During the COVID-19 pandemic, which caused many places to shut down, Joe learned to improvise. Even though regular team workouts were canceled, he took the lead and organized teammates to meet up unofficially, so that they could make sure they stayed fit. Improvisation is key to success in both football and life.

- In 2020, Joe sustained a bad injury to his knee, which threatened to end his career. It was certainly a terrible blow, but Joe took it all in stride. He cooperated with doctors, underwent surgery, and then did his best to recuperate. This sustained focus on recovery saw him come back stronger than ever. Joe learned that it's not so much about getting knocked down, but how you get back up.

AARON RODGERS
THE FINE ART OF FOOTBALL

Aaron Rodgers is one of the best football players the NFL has ever seen. He was born on December 2, 1983, in Chico, California, to Edward and Darla Rodgers, and football was a favorite family pastime. His dad played football in college, and Aaron grew up playing ball with his father. When he was just a toddler, he watched entire football games on television, from beginning to end.

As much as he liked football, Aaron's first love was basketball. He was just 10 years old when he was featured in the *Ukiah Daily Journal*. The article mentioned his skills at a local basketball tournament. But big changes were in store for young Aaron Rodgers when his family decided to move north from Chico, California, to Beaverton, Oregon.

Aaron finished up elementary school in Beaverton, and then went on to Whitford Middle School, where he played baseball on the Little League team. But then the family moved back to Chico, where Aaron attended Pleasant Valley High. There, he honed his budding football skills, and eventually the high school's quarterback. Aaron set multiple records at Pleasant Valley, including the single-season record for total yards (2466).

During his time at Pleasant Valley High, Aaron was not only a good football player, but also an excellent student who earned straight As and attained a high score on his SATs. Even without football, Aaron most certainly seemed like college material.

However, he had a hard time generating any attention from Division I football recruiters.

Aaron graduated from Pleasant Valley in 2002. Instead of immediately attending one of the major colleges, he set his sights on a small community college not far from Chico—Butte College. Aaron was discouraged that NFL recruiters didn't seem to take too much notice of him, and considered enrolling in law school to pursue a career as a professional attorney. But he also remained committed to excellence on the field. During his freshman year at Butte, he threw 26 touchdown passes and finished the season with a very impressive 10-1 record.

Riding high on these great stats, Aaron Rodgers transferred to the University of California in Berkley. He hit the ground running during the 2003 season, and by his fifth game he was the team's starting quarterback. At the end of his sophomore year, he had led the team to a 7-3 record. He did even better his junior year, finishing the season with a 10-1 record.

Aaron Rodgers was drafted into the NFL in 2005 as the 24th pick, signing with the Green Bay Packers. The team gave him a five-year, $7.7 million contract. Green Bay already had a star quarterback at the time by way of NFL veteran Brett Favre, and Aaron was signed as a backup to Brett. He had some fairly big shoes to fill, but he was determined to do his best.

The problem was that he was rarely allowed out onto the field. He was able to show his stuff here and there, such as during the fourth quarter of a game against the New Orleans Saints, but didn't get any regular playing time.

At the end of that first season, the Packers decided to get rid of Coach Mike Sherman, in favor of a new head coach—Mike McCarthy. McCarthy took a closer look at Aaron and decided to further finesse the skills of this new quarterback by having him participate in what was known as "quarterback school." This consisted of having Rodgers train for six hours a day, several days a week, working on special techniques that would help him to become a better quarterback.

This special training put an emphasis on seemingly minor—yet incredibly important—details of how Aaron played the game. For example, Aaron tended to release the ball too soon. Coach McCarthy sought to correct this flaw by refining Rodgers' release point, so that he would not release the ball when it was lined up with the ear hole of his helmet, but rather when it was further behind and below it.

As detailed as this refinement might have been, Aaron took his lessons to heart and was soon playing better than ever before. Meanwhile, many Packers fans were openly speculating about whether Brett Favre might be ready to retire soon.

No one wondered about this more than Aaron Rodgers, who was expected to eventually take the veteran's place. Favre dispelled any such speculation, however, when he announced that he would stay on until the 2007 season. The following year, in 2008, Favre left the Packers, which meant Aaron finally had the starting position.

Aaron was now the new face of Packers football, and he didn't want to disappoint his fans. He tried hard, and his performances over the next couple of seasons were notable. In fact, after a stellar 2010 season, Aaron led his team all the way to the Super Bowl. On February 6, 2011, the Packers scored a major victory over the Pittsburgh Steelers, winning 31-25.

Aaron played several more great seasons with the Packers before being traded to the New York Jets in 2023.

FIVE FUN FACTS

- Aaron Rodgers was drafted into the NFL in 2005.
- He began his time with the Packers as a backup for Brett Favre.
- He's been named NFL MVP three times.
- Aaron Rodgers and the Packers won Super Bowl XLV.
- Aaron is a vegetarian.

SOME TRIVIA!

Does he have any hobbies?

Music is his hobby. In fact, Aaron Rodgers plays a mean guitar.

What does Aaron Rodgers do when he throws a touchdown pass?

He puts on his invisible "championship belt." Aaron has been known to be quite an imaginative character, and he acts as if he is putting a belt around his waist after scoring touchdowns. Yes, it's silly, but fans love him for it.

What game show did Aaron Rodgers appear on as a guest host?

Jeopardy.

What Wisconsin product has Rodgers cut out of his diet?

It might be a bit ironic, since he used to be a "Cheesehead", but vegetarian Aaron Rodgers has sworn off the consumption of cheese.

What famous baseball player is Aaron Rodgers friends with?

Aaron is buddies with Milwaukee Brewers player Ryan Braun.

REAL-LIFE LESSONS

- Aaron Rodgers had a keen interest in sports from an early age. He was also able to pay attention and not get distracted. Early on, he learned to be laser-focused on football and anything else that gained his attention. We should all learn to focus on what's important to us.

- During his early years with the Green Bay Packers, Aaron learned what a difference a coach can make. The Packers switched out their old coach, Mike Sherman, for Mike McCarthy, and the difference was like night and day. McCarthy had faith in Aaron Rodgers, and the two forged a lasting bond that greatly contributed to Aaron's success. We would all be wise to recognize solid partnerships like this in our lives.

- Aaron Rodgers spent time refining his technique. He corrected bad habits he had developed, which helped him play better. We should also strive to do the same in the things that are important to us.

- During all of the speculation over whether or not Packers quarterback Brett Favre would retire, Aaron remained patient. He knew his time would come—he just had to wait until his moment. It would do us all a little good to learn patience like this.

- After he became the official starting quarterback for the Packers, Aaron knew that a lot of Packers fans were eager to see him succeed. But he didn't let the pressure get to him. Instead, he just kept his head down and did his job. Steadfast determination like this is a good lesson to learn.

ROB GRONKOWSKI
IT'S GOTTA BE GRONK

Rob Gronkowski is a unique talent. Similar to J.J. Watt, he's a big guy who can make some major moves. Hard to tackle and outmaneuver, he was the nearly indestructible glue that held many of his team's plays together.

Rob was born on May 14, 1989, in Amherst, New York, to Diane and Gordon Gronkowski. Rob's dad was himself a football star back in his day, having played for Syracuse University in the late 1970s and early 1980s.

The family made their way to the suburbs of Pittsburgh in 2006. While there, Rob played football for Woodland Hills High during his senior year. He graduated with honors and a 3.75 grade point average in 2007, and was well on his way to college and a successful football career.

Rob attended the University of Arizona, playing as a tight end for the school's football team. His freshman season, he logged 28 receptions for 525 yards and scored six touchdowns. He also had an average of 18.8 yards per reception, which, at that time, was the top statistic for the team.

The 2008 season was a bit less consistent for Rob. He missed three games in a row at the start of the season, but he eventually rallied and managed to score several touchdowns by the end of the year. At one point, he was also named the John Mackey

National Tight End of the Week. The 2009 season was even better, and in 2010, Rob was drafted into the NFL by the New England Patriots.

Rob immediately proved how valuable he could be for an NFL team. In particular, he demonstrated how in sync he was with Patriots quarterback Tom Brady. During week 10 of that season, in a game against the Pittsburgh Steelers, Rob caught three touchdown passes from Brady. This was an NFL record for a rookie to accomplish this so early in their career.

The 2011 season was even more memorable for Rob and the Patriots, as they made it to the Super Bowl. With mere seconds remaining in the game, Rob found himself at the receiving end of a last-ditch Hail Mary pass from Tom Brady. All eyes were on Rob as he dived for the ball, but the pass was incomplete. The Patriots ended up losing to the New York Giants 21 to 17.

There were more opportunities, however, with Rob Gronkowski and Tom Brady leading the Patriots to Super Bowl victories in 2015, 2017, and 2019. Then, deciding to go out on top, Rob announced his retirement from football a short time later.

As good as his football career was, Rob's attempt at retirement proved to be a flop. As soon as he announced that he was done with football, he seemed to have second thoughts. Instead of retiring, he started the 2020 season with the Tampa Bay Buccaneers. This was an interesting decision, since Tom Brady had been traded to the Buccaneers, as well.

The dynamic football duo was reunited on another team, and they proved that their formidable collaboration was limited to the Patriots. The Buccaneers made it to the Super Bowl that year, where they hammered the Kansas City Chiefs, 31-9. Rob then played one more season for the Buccaneers before announcing his final retirement from the game on June 21, 2022.

FIVE FUN FACTS

- Rob loves horses. In fact, there's a race horse that is officially named "Gronkowski" in his honor.
- Rob Gronkowski once appeared as a wrestler in the WWE.
- He has appeared in five Pro Bowls.
- He holds the record for most touchdowns by a tight end in a single season.
- His memoir "It's Good to be Gronk" is a New York Times best seller.

SOME TRIVIA!

Does he have a nickname?

Yes, everyone calls him "Gronk."

What is the Gronk Spike?

The Gronk Spike is the celebratory celebration that Rob engages in after a touchdown.

How many times has Rob retired from football?

Twice.

How many Super Bowl rings does he have?

He has four Super Bowl rings.

Does he have a hobby?

Gronk enjoys weight lifting.

REAL-LIFE LESSONS

- Rob knew the importance of being a well-rounded individual. He made sure to do just as well in academics as he did in football. He graduated from high school with a 3.74 grade point average.

- Gronk is known for his physical strength, but also he proved his mental and emotional resilience during difficult times. Soon after Rob left home for college, his parents split up. The turbulence of his personal life wasn't easy, but he learned to rise above it. By the end of his first college football season, he was doing well both on and off the field.
- Gronkowski was disappointed in 2012 when, during the final moments of the Super Bowl, quarterback Tom Brady's Hail Mary long pass failed to connect. But he knew he had to make the best of it and move on. That's a good lesson for all of us to learn.
- Rob Gronkowski played football with star quarterback Tom Brady, and learned the value of a tight partnership. These two knew each other so well that they were an almost unbeatable combination. If you find a winning combination like this, be sure to make use of it.
- In 2019, Gronkowski announced to the world that he was retiring. The following year, however, he revealed that he had changed his mind and would instead play for the Tampa Bay Buccaneers, with his old friend Tom Brady. Rob knew that it was okay to change his mind. Just because we think something one day doesn't mean that we can't change our trajectory the next.

KICKING IT WITH ADAM VINATIERI

It's usually the quarterback who gets the most attention in a football game. The place kicker, on the other hand, doesn't get much hype. But that wasn't the case with the long and celebrated career of Adam Vinatieri.

Adam began life in Yankton, South Dakota, where he was born to Judy and Paul Vinatieri on December 28, 1972. When Adam was just five years old, his family decided to move to Rapid City, South Dakota, where the boy began his formal education. He didn't have an easy go of it. Early on, Adam struggled with various learning disabilities. Nevertheless, he proved how resilient he was and learned how to adapt. He also picked up sports.

Adam played football for Central High in Rapid City. In the early days, he actually played as a quarterback. But after high school, it took him some time to figure out what he really wanted to do.

Initially, he headed off to the US military academy at West Point. It took just a couple of weeks there to realize that military life was not for him. He then signed up for classes at South Dakota State University, where he once again played football. This time, he played as a kicker and punter. He later remarked that the switch was largely due to the fact that he was much smaller than most other quarterbacks. A position as a kicker just seemed more fitting for him and his particular build skillset.

After college, Adam was drafted by the New England Patriots in 1996. He initially signed on as an undrafted free agent, but very early in the season, he began to make a name for himself. He became particularly well known for being able to make conversions. In the NFL, a conversion is the field goal attempt made after a touchdown. As was the case during a memorable match up against the Jacksonville, Jaguars, when a conversion, managed to eke out a 28 to 25 win against the Patriots.

One of the most impressive moments in his career came during Super Bowl XXXVIII, on February 1, 2004. With just seconds left on the clock, Adam kicked a field goal from the 41-yard line, securing the win for the Patriots.

Adam went on to prove that he was a valuable player no matter where he played. He was picked up by Indianapolis, and worked the same magic for the Colts for many seasons before he ultimately retired on May 26, 2021. Although he started his career with the rival of the Indianapolis Colts—the New England Patriots—Adam Vinatieri is universally loved by Colts fans. He has often returned the love, and will always have a soft spot in his heart for Indianapolis and the strong fanbase he has there.

FIVE FUN FACTS

- Adam left the New England Patriots for the Indianapolis Colts in 2006.
- He has more Super Bowl rings than any other NFL kicker.
- Adam played for South Dakota State.
- He is the oldest player to have scored more than 100 points in a single season.
- He has played in more playoff games than anyone else in the NFL.

SOME TRIVIA!

How many Super Bowl rings does he have?

Adam has four Super Bowl rings.

What unique football record does Adam hold?

Adam has a record for most field goals in NFL playoff history.

Does he have a hobby?

Yes, he enjoys hunting.

Does he have a nickname?

Yes! He's so consistent with his field goal kicks that fans call him "Automatic Adam."

What is his favorite food?

He loves to eat big-game animals, such as the deer that he hunts.

REAL-LIFE LESSONS

- Adam Vinatieri proved that it's not only the quarterback who can steal the show in football, since he gained widespread attention for his efforts as a place kicker. As Adam demonstrates, it's not so much the position we're given, but how we make use of it that matters.

- Growing up, Adam Vinatieri struggled with learning disabilities. He had his challenges, but he found ways to adapt and overcome them. He applied this same resiliency to the football field and everything else he did. We should all try to do the same!
- After graduating from high school, it took Adam a while to figure out what he wanted to do. There is nothing wrong with taking time to consider one's options. Life is a learning process, and sometimes we have to explore various avenues to find our ultimate path.
- Adam initially played football as a quarterback, in college he made the switch to place kicker, since he was smaller than most other players and seemed better suited for the role. It was just a hunch, but Adam went with his gut feeling and it worked out incredibly well. Don't be afraid to experiment, in football or anything else in life.

CONCLUSION
IT'S HOW YOU PLAY THE GAME

Football may be only a game to some, but for others, it's their life. If you want to do really well in football, you have to have the right mindset. You have to know how to be a team player, you have to be strategic in your approach, and you have to set goals to work toward

All of the players featured in this book learned how to be disciplined and hard-working individuals who contributed to their teams and achieved spectacular things. They all have different strengths and weaknesses, but learned valuable lessons during their careers.

Jerome Bettis learned how to live (and play football) with asthma. For those who don't suffer from asthma, this might not seem like a big thing, but it was actually a huge deal.

Brett Favre, on the other hand, learned the valuable lesson of not taking anything for granted. He had just started his football career when a terrible car accident almost upended it. He was lucky he was still able to play ball—in fact, he was lucky he was still alive. From that day forward, Brett counted every day he was still breathing as a good one.

Most importantly, all of these players have learned that scoring points and winning games isn't everything. It is possible to lose a game—as Peyton Manning did in his first Super Bowl with the Broncos—and still come out as a real winner by demonstrating graciousness in defeat. On the other hand, someone could win big, as Travis Kelce did in the Super Bowl in 2024, yet behave so poorly that the world looks down on them. Much more important than winning or losing—both in the game of football and the game of life—is how you play the game.

BONUS SECTION AFFIRMATIONS TO HELP YOUNG ATHLETES IMPROVE CONFIDENCE AND THEIR MENTAL GAME

1. I will do well.

2. I will work hard.

3. I will succeed.

4. I will believe in myself.

5. I will have good intentions.

6. I will listen to coaches/instructors.

7. I will be a team player.

8. I will be kind.

9. I won't take anything for granted.

10. I will be respectful.

11. I will be considerate.

12. I will be strong.

13. I will be dedicated.

14. I will be resilient.

15. I will be trustworthy.

16. I will keep a routine schedule.

17. I will be creative.

18. Each day, I will remind myself to do good.

19. I will live in the present.

20. I will love myself.

21. I am ready to change/adapt if necessary.

22. I am proud of myself.

23. I will enjoy every moment.

24. I can shape my own destiny.

25. I will keep an open mind.

26. I am happy and fulfilled.

27. I will make my dreams come true.

28. I have unique talents to offer.

29. I will focus on what's important.

30. I will balance life, both on and off the field.

31. I will seize opportunity.

32. I will do the best I can.

33. I will be a team player.

34. I will collaborate with others.

35. I will become what I am destined to be.

36. The future has great things in store for me.

37. I will maintain a positive attitude.

38. I will forgive myself for my failings.

39. I will forgive the failings of others.

40. I will be tolerant of others.

41. I will receive constructive criticism.

42. I will help others to improve.

43. I will maintain self-control.

44. I will persevere.

45. I will show strength in the face of adversity.

46. I will rise to the challenge.

47. I will be resilient

48. I will be prosperous.

49. I will speak the truth.

50. I will keep an open mind.

51. I will follow my gut feelings.

52. I will be patient with others.

53. I will be courteous.

54. I will practice and train regularly.

55. I will look forward to the future.

56. I will be a major asset to the team.

57. I will score points on the field and in life.

58. I will get back up when knocked down.

59. I will make the best of any situation.

60. I will recognize the talents of others.

61. I will forge dynamic partnerships.

62. I will always look out for my teammates.

63. I will listen to the coach.

64. I will keep focused on the game.

65. I won't let anything slow me down.

66. I'll have a positive attitude.

67. I'll be friendly to others.

68. I'll always be on time.

69. I'll stay mentally sharp and physically fit.

70. I'll exercise every day.

71. I'll throw the football better than ever.

72. I'll wear my jersey with pride.

73. I'll be grateful for every game.

74. I'll never have second thoughts.

75. I'll do my absolute best.

76. I'll keep things in perspective.

77. I'll pay attention to details.

78. I'll rest when I need to.

79. I'll make sure to stay healthy.

80. I'll have a good diet and exercise routine.

81. I'll plan the future carefully.

82. I'll take things as they come.

83. I'll give the game everything I've got.

84. I'll take time to breathe.

85. I'll enjoy the moment.

86. I'll keep things focused.

87. I won't make any excuses.

88. I'll keep it simple.

89. I won't stress out over minor details.

90. I'll see the big picture.

91. I'll practice all my plays.

92. I'll run faster than anyone.

93. I'll catch every ball.

94. I'll throw further than ever before.

95. I'll be a fountain of energy.

96. I'll make it to the big time.

97. I'll make good choices in life.

98. I'll play like a pro.

99. I'm a champion.

100. I know what I'm doing.

101. I'm the best at what I do.

102. I have all the skills necessary.

103. I'm in it to win it.

104. I will be good in good time.

105. My mind is sharp.

106. It's going to be a great game.

107. Life is what you make it.

108. Football is my passion.

109. I love playing the game.

110. I've trained well.

111. I'm laser-focused.

112. I have what it takes.

113. It's going to be a great day.

114. Football is fun.

115. I have a long time to learn.

116. There's nothing better than doing well.

117. I feel good.

118. I'm going to succeed.

119. This is going to be great.

120. We're in this together.

121. We can do it.

122. I'm growing all the time.

123. I'm sending good feelings to everyone.

124. I love being around my teammates.

125. I'm happy when others do well.

126. There's room for all of us to grow.

127. I value sportsmanlike conduct.

128. I will be polite.

129. Good things will come in good time.

130. I will affirm and encourage my teammates.

131. I am not afraid to ask for help.

132. I am content and free from despair.

133. I am a unique and gifted person.

134. I have a valuable skillset to offer.

135. I am loved and supported by others.

136. I alone control my destiny.

137. I am at peace.

138. I am responsible for my own actions.

139. I will learn as I grow.

140. I will rest when necessary.

141. I look for the good in others.

142. I will take my time.

143. I am not afraid of change.

144. I have everything I could possibly need.

145. I look forward to the next game.

146. I am not afraid.

147. I am fully capable.

148. I appreciate the wisdom of others.

149. I have kind words for my teammates.

150. I am worthy of love and kindness.

151. I have a unique perspective.

152. My emotions are my own.

153. There is a place for me on the team.

154. I serve a unique purpose.

155. Life is rewarding.

156. I am excited to start the day.

157. I can meet any challenge.

158. I am my number one fan.

159. I can achieve my goals.

160. I am confident.

161. I will pick myself up when I fall.

162. I can adapt to changes.

163. I have a great purpose to fulfill.

164. My destiny is great.

165. Great things are in store.

166. I will work harder than ever.

167. I will commit myself to my team.

168. I will always do everything I can.

169. My teammates will help me.

170. I won't harbor any ill will to anyone.

171. I will be positive at all times.

172. I will make the best of any situation.

173. I will be happy when others succeed.

174. I won't hold grudges.

175. I will be a positive influence on the team.

176. I am increasingly fulfilled.

177. I have inner peace.

178. I am not easily panicked.

179. I am in sync with my teammates.

180. I have the right to enjoy myself.

181. I'm not afraid to speak my mind.

182. I can meet people half way.

183. I am open-minded.

184. I can entertain the views of others.

185. Life is full of opportunity.

186. The future shines bright.

187. I am bold and courageous.

188. I won't back down.

189. I'm open to change and opportunity.

190. I will not dwell on the past.

191. I am willing to help others.

192. I have faith in myself.

193. I am in control of my thoughts.

194. I will choose wisely.

195. Life is good.

196. The team is getting better all the time.

197. There is still much work to do.

198. I will play like a champion.

199. I will be prepared.

200. I will score a touchdown.

201. I will intercept the ball.

202. I won't get sacked!

203. I will stand tall and unintimidated.

204. I will be everything I need to be.

205. I will learn to roll with the punches.

206. I will listen to the coach!

207. I will pay attention to my surroundings.

208. I will always do my best.

209. I am up for a challenge.

210. I will keep everything in focus.

211. I am the best at what I do.

212. I have a lot to look forward to.

213. The future is bright.

214. Football is fun.

215. I will be happy with what I do.

216. I will learn as I go.

217. I won't compromise my integrity.

218. I will use my imagination.

219. I will breathe deep and remain calm.

220. I will focus on what's important.

221. I will keep it real.

222. I will always be up for the challenge.

223. I will learn to work with others.

224. I will grow my talent.

225. I won't get tired.

226. I will stay strong.

227. I will come out on top.

228. I will see things through.

229. I will win.

230. I will find a way to succeed.

231. I will navigate through life.

232. I will never forget those who love me.

233. I will keep going.

234. I will remain in place.

235. I won't falter.

236. I won't complain.

237. I'll keep it steady.

238. I will perform well.

239. I'll learn from my mistakes.

240. I'll teach others.

241. I am enough.

242. I'll get through life's challenges.

243. I've overcome many obstacles.

244. I will feel good.

245. I will help others achieve their goals.

246. I will be a good example.

247. I'll collaborate with my teammates.

248. I'll always look on the bright side.

249. I won't get tackled.

250. I'll be all that I can be.

251. I'll stand tall.

252. I won't quit.

253. Every day is a new possibility.

254. I'm safe and secure.

255. I have no problems, only solutions.

256. I will work with others.

257. I will get stronger.

258. I will become more determined every day.

259. I will not dim the light within me.

260. I am in the right place at the right time.

261. My heart is my anchor.

262. I am loved as I am.

263. I will love and be loved.

264. I will let my light shine.

265. My voice will be heard.

266. I will work harder than ever before.

267. I will drink in my happiness.

268. I am good enough.

269. I work in steady deliberation.

270. My life is amazing.

271. I am making a difference.

272. I have a unique perspective.

273. It's going to be a good day.

274. I will increase with time.

275. My knowledge is great.

276. I am worth it.

277. No harm will come to me.

278. Hope springs eternal.

279. Life is a gift.

280. Football is a privilege.

281. I will think big.

282. I will embrace who I am.

283. I am an integral part of a team.

284. Every day is a celebration.

285. I am not afraid to grow.

286. Everything is possible.

287. I will set my mind to great things.

288. I will keep my head up.

289. I will remain confident.

290. I will improve my mental game.

291. I will keep on task.

292. I will play like I mean it.

293. Every throw will connect.

294. Every pass will succeed.

295. I will be victorious.

296. I will run at full speed.

297. There will be no hesitation.

298. I will be blessed.

299. I will have everything I need.

300. I will pass every test.

301. No matter what, I will make it through.

302. I will know what to do.

303. It's going to be a great season.

304. Football is for me.

305. Life is fulfilling.

306. I get meaning from every breath.

307. I am willing to do my very best.

308. I will chart my own course.

309. I will listen to others.

310. I will give back.

311. I will tune my heart to what is right.

312. I will keep a clear mind.

313. I will wake up ready to go.

314. I will be intentional and consistent.

315. I will show initiative.

316. I will be modest and not boast.

317. I will think the best of others.

318. I choose faith over fear.

319. I invite feelings of warmth and joy.

320. I will turn away from negativity.

321. I will not complain.

322. I will have a glad heart.

323. I will focus on the good.

324. I will be a good example for my team.

325. I will set and reach my goals.

326. The end zone is within my reach.

327. It's going to be a great season.

328. I will make the playoffs.

329. I will develop endurance.

330. I will earn respect from my peers.

331. I will be a good competitor.

332. My training will pay off.

333. I'm going to take things to the next level.

THE MENTAL MINDSET TO HELP YOU SUCCEED IN FOOTBALL

Football is a game that requires the right kind of mindset in order to succeed. The game can be challenging at times, but developing the right kind of mindset early on will help to ensure objectives are met.

AFFIRMATIONS

Successful football players need to be confident in themselves and their ability to play the sport. Having that said, affirmations are a great way to engage in confidence building. Affirmations can be spoken out loud or simply read from a page. Positive words of encouragement such as those presented in this book are crucial in building up a confident and capable mindset.

FACE YOUR EMOTIONS

Emotions are all part of the human experience. Without emotions we simply wouldn't be human—*we would be machines*. But it's also the fact that we humans can control our emotions which separates us from wild animals which might bite first and think later. And as it pertains to football, we are best served when we are able to control our emotions. This doesn't mean we ignore our emotions; it just means that we are able to control how we express them. We might not like a certain call made by the referee for example, but hurling the football in the ref's face out of anger is not going to help anyone! We need to take ownership of our own emotions at all times.

SET GOALS

Keep your mind focused, and set attainable goals for yourself. It's always good to be able to set and meet goals, in order to gauge your own personal growth. The more goals you meet, the better you will feel about your own progress.

BE A TEAM PLAYER

Football requires teamwork. Having the mindset of a team player therefore is critical to success on the football field. If you don't have that much experience playing on a team, you can gain a sense of teamwork simply by cooperating, with friends, family, or even your neighbors. Helping a neighbor with yard work for example, is an excellent example of teamwork. It's this mindset of cooperation that needs to be cultivated in order to be a true team player both on and off the field.

ACKNOWLEDGE THERE IS ALWAYS MORE TO LEARN

We live and we learn. We need to simply humble ourselves and acknowledge that we don't know everything. For the more open we are to learning, the better we will become. We should also be open to the criticism of others and willing to correct errors as we go.

THE TEAMS

Football is played on a football field. Each end of the field is called the "end zone." The game starts with one team on the offensive, in possession of the football and trying to break through the other team's defense, so that they can reach the end zone on the other side. If the team with the ball manages to struggle their way to the endzone, they score what's called a touchdown. Teams can also score points by kicking the football through a field goal.

EQUIPMENT

Football equipment primarily consists of protective padding, football uniforms, gloves, mouthguards, football helmets, and the football itself.

PLAYING BASICS

Football consists of pitting two teams against each other with one on the offense and the other on the defense. There are several positions in football. The offensive team is led by the quarterback who initiates plays. The quarterback throws the ball to receivers, as they attempt to get further in reach of the endzone. The team on the defense utilizes several defensive positions such as linebackers who do everything they can to keep the offensive team from moving the ball further down the field.

RULES TO KEEP IN MIND

Football is fun but it has plenty of rules to keep in mind. To develop a good mindset for the game, it would be wise to learn how to follow them.

Some of the most important rules are:

- The main objective of the game is for a team to reach their opponent's end zone to score a touchdown.
- Touchdowns are worth 6 points.
- Field goals are worth 3 points.
- An extra point is given for a field goal made after a touchdown.
- A football game is broken up into 4 fifteen minute quarters.

Made in the USA
Columbia, SC
17 December 2024

49840526R00072